Oscar Browning

I Presume
H.M. Stanley's Triumph and Disaster (Bles, 1956)

The Knight and the Umbrella
An account of the Eglinton Tournament (Bles, 1963)

The Scandal of the Andover Workhouse
(Bles, 1973)

Oscar Browning

A BIOGRAPHY

Ian Anstruther

JOHN MURRAY

© Ian Anstruther 1983

First published 1983
by John Murray (Publishers) Ltd
50 Albemarle Street, London W1X 4BD

Typeset by Inforum Ltd, Portsmouth
Printed and bound in Great Britain
by The Pitman Press, Bath

British Library Cataloguing in Publication Data
Anstruther, Ian
Oscar Browning.
1. Browning, Oscar   2. Teachers—Biography
I. Title
371.1'0092'4   LA2377.B/
ISBN 0–7195–4078–X

Contents

Acknowledgements   ix

Preface   1

I   Introducing the dilemma   5

II   Eton, King's, and Eton   12

III   In loco parentis   20

IV   The 'violent reformer'   45

V   Greek love and George Curzon   55

VI   'Ruined and disgraced'   67

VII   Colleagues, clubs, and Sunday 'sociables'   81

VIII   The patron of youth   93

IX   The man of the day   103

X   Family affairs, and Robbie Ross   121

XI   'Well and fat and not too amorous'   138

XII   The paedagogue seeks the Holy Grail   149

XIII   Dropping the pilot   163

XIV   Oscar Browning, O.B.E.   180

Postscript   189

Appendix A   Pusey on masturbation   192

Appendix B   List of Portraits, etc. of Oscar Browning   193

Notes   195

Bibliography and sources   198

Index   205

Illustrations

1 Browning aged about four   *f.p.* 38

2 Browning aged twenty-two   38

3 George Curzon at Eton   39

4 Curzon and Browning in 1878   39

5 Eton in the late 19th Century   54

6 Browning and Hornby: contemporary cartoon   54

7 Browning in the 1890s   55

8 Browning with Day Training College Students   118

9 'Mid-Term Tea at Mr Oscar Brownings',

   by Max Beerbohm   118

10 Browning by Ignazio Zuloaga   119

11 Senate House and tricycle   134

12 The Backs   134

13 Browning by Emanuel Gliecenstein   135

Contemporary cartoons of Oscar Browning will be found throughout the text. That on p viii is from *Friends In Pencil*, a Cambridge Sketch Book, 1893. The rest are from *The Granta*: p11, 9 May 1896; p44, 2 March 1895; p80, 17 October 1896; p148, 26 October 1901; p194, May Week number, 1902; p204, 28 October 1899

ILLUSTRATION CREDITS

1, Mrs T.K. Irvine; 2, the Master and Fellows of Trinity College, Cambridge; 3, 5, 6, the Provost and Fellows of Eton College; 4, from *Memories of Sixty Years* by Oscar Browning; 7, Frank Lumley Esq.; 8, Department of Education, University of Cambridge; 9, 10, the Provost and Fellows of King's College, Cambridge; 11, May Week Supplement to *The Grunter*, 1920, Cambridgeshire Collection, Central Library, Cambridge; 12, Cambridge University Library; 13, Joseph Leftwich Esq.

"LUNCH," OR "THE CAMBRIDGE CAVIARE."

Acknowledgements

Necessarily, the help and advice of many people is required for the preparation of a book of this kind. Once the script is complete and approved by the publisher, to acknowledge their assistance remains a last duty and real pleasure. Firstly, therefore, I thank Her Majesty the Queen for gracious permission to quote the letter of June 1st 1918, from Oscar Browning to Queen Mary. Secondly, I thank the Provost and Fellows of Eton College; of King's College, Cambridge; and the Master and Fellows of Trinity College, Cambridge for permission to work in their splendid libraries; and also the Master and Fellows of Magdalene College, Cambridge, for sanction to read and quote from the Diaries of A.C. Benson. I thank the staff of the University Library, Cambridge, especially Patricia Aske in the Rare Books department, for their skilled and friendly help; the Department of Education, University of Cambridge, for permission to study and quote from their archives; also the Clerk to the Cambridge Union Debating Society for giving me access to the Society's Minute Books. Without the authority of these august bodies and learned custodians the book could not have been done in its present form. Thirdly, I acknowledge with sincere gratitude all those people who helped me in ways which perhaps to them was a trifling matter but to me was very important: The Rt Hon William Deedes PC; The Rev. Dr Peter Newman Brooks; Patrick Wilkinson; Christopher Morris; Michael Halls; Kenneth Timings; Kenneth Rose; Lionel Lambourne; Jeremy Potter; Joseph Leftwich; Emanuele Romano; Timothy d'Arch Smith and John Murray, Sr, who knows as only a publisher can do, what his support has meant to me.

More than one hundred people answered my advertisements for letters and photographs connected with O.B. I thank them once more, especially those who sent me letters from boys who

Acknowledgements

were at O.B.'s house at Eton. Many of O.B.'s great-nephews and nieces wrote to me – I thank them particularly – most of all Mrs Berta Wortham, the custodian of the copyright of all O.B.'s unpublished letters, without whose consent this book could not have been published. I thank the Chief Librarian of the East Sussex County Council which owns the Browning Archive, and the Principal Librarian of the Eastbourne Central Library which at present houses the Archive, for giving me unfettered access to it; Maureen Holden for patient research there on my behalf; also the Secretary and staff of the Royal Commission on Historical Manuscripts whose work, covering a period of ten years, produced its faultless index. I thank formally, once more: The Earl of Balfour; The Viscount Scarsdale; The Lord Walston; Commander J. Goodford; Lieut. Colonel A.J. Clark Kennedy; Patrick Furse, Esq.; Charles Crawley, Esq.; Francis Warre Cornish, Esq.; Mrs Janet Stone; Miss Eleanor Hamilton Thompson; for permission to use their family papers. More personally, I thank David Newsome for letting me use his index to A.C. Benson's Diaries – an act of real kindness. With real gratitude I thank my secretary, Barbara Copeland, who has supervised the preparation of this book from first to last with impeccable patience and ability.

Finally, I thank Dr Peter Searby, Fellow of Fitzwilliam College, Cambridge, Lecturer in nineteenth-century history at the University's Department of Education; Dr Patrick Strong, Eton College Archivist; and his wife, Felicity, formerly Registrar at the National Register of Archives. Their kindness in guiding me in their own special fields (not to speak of their hospitality) has been truly immeasurable.

Sally Bicknell has done the index. I thank her warmly.

Though every care has been taken, if through inadvertence or failure to trace the present owners, I have included any copyright material without acknowledgement or permission, I offer my apologies to all concerned.

Preface

Anyone writing a book about Oscar Browning is faced immediately with one outstanding problem. This is the amount of material in the Browning Archive which contains letters from at least 10,000 correspondents. In all, there are something like 50,000 letters – for Browning was a man who kept everything, however trivial. He was at the same time, an assiduous correspondent, even by Victorian standards, rising every morning at six o'clock to drink tea and write twenty or thirty letters of great length, swiftly and illegibly, before he began the normal work for the day. So, of course, he received a very large number of letters in return. These he filed carefully in alphabetical order in cardboard boxes which lay for fifty years, from 1917 to 1967, undisturbed in the Hastings Public Library to which he had given them. Then, their interest being realised, they were taken to London to be listed by the Royal Commission on Historical Manuscripts.

There are nearly 2,000 letters from boy-soldiers and sailors, and other less reputable young men with whom he had a mixture of pure and impure relationships; 750 from his lifelong friend Frank Money-Coutts; 700 from his sisters; 526 from Sir George Prothero, a colleague at King's; 480 from Fred Harvey, a secretary known as 'Piggy'; 340 from a Mr and Mrs Featonby Smith. So the list goes on. Added to which there are perhaps as many as 10,000 letters at Cambridge and elsewhere from official correspondents in the world of education.

The problem these letters sets to the biographer is immense. Clearly, to read them all is impossible; yet they must be glanced at in the first instance, at least; and then indexed and cross-indexed for further study at a later date when the work has begun to reveal its final requirements. My hope is that, in spite of inevitable omissions with an archive of this size, I have not left out anything important. I have not said anything, for example, about Browning's work for the Evening Classes Association in Cambridge concerning which there are more than 300 letters; nor on a more personal level, anything about his correspondence with that interesting woman, Charlotte Mason, founder of the PNEU. Nevertheless I trust I have succeeded, as I have tried hard to do, in presenting a balanced and just portrait of him. He was, by any standard, a remarkable man.

For SEBASTIAN

CHAPTER I

Introducing the dilemma

In September 1875, the miniature world of Eton College suddenly found itself in the news when one of its masters, Oscar Browning, was given notice of dismissal. The reason for this appeared to be obscure. Browning was known to have been a rebel and not to get on with the school's headmaster, but no one had ever guessed for a moment that Dr Hornby would try to sack him. Such a thing had not been done since Nicholas Udall, in the sixteenth century, had gone to prison for the crime of buggery. Browning's fault, in comparison, was slight. He had merely broken a regulation concerning the number of boys he was tutoring. The maximum number permitted was forty. Browning was tutoring forty-three. He had exceeded the limit previously for several periods with Dr Hornby's express permission, but on this occasion he had assumed consent, and had most unwisely failed to ask for it. Dr Hornby had taken umbrage and, it seemed, in a fit of temper, had peremptorily dismissed him.

In the ordinary way a master's dismissal, even dismissal from Eton College, could not be considered of national interest; but in Browning's case it was different. He was then aged thirty-eight, had been a master for fifteen years, and his house was said, at least by some – by those who believed that a schoolboy's life should not be entirely a matter of games – to be quite the best of any in the country. Thus he was known to a host of people, from William Gladstone to dashing officers in furthest Poona whose sons were expecting to go to his house. For he was, in fact, a part of Eton, the largest public school in the country; a part of the great national system which educated boys to govern the Empire, a system approved by Parliament itself in recent legislation.

So people demanded: what had happened? For a man on the brink of middle-age could not possibly be sent away from such a place as Eton College after many years of admirable service with no pension and no prospect just for having too many pupils. Something serious must be behind it.

Browning's account of the Eton disaster, told in his *Memories of Sixty Years*, related the facts without the background; so does his nephew, Hugo Wortham, who with the help of his uncle's diary (now lost, perhaps destroyed) wrote his life in 1927. The facts appeared simply to be these: that Browning had, by a 'pure oversight', forgotten to obtain the required permission to continue taking the extra pupils. Dr Hornby, quite unreasonably, had taken this as a personal challenge. Having the support of the Governing Body, Hornby had made up his mind to sack him, quite regardless of anything else: the possible inconvenience to parents, the certain destruction of Browning's career. The true facts, however, were different, and much more devious and complex than either Browning or Wortham disclosed. Dr Hornby had faced a dilemma. Browning went in for passionate friendships – in the phrase of the time, indulged in spooning – in having pets and making favourites; not only with boys who were pretty or clever who boarded with him in his own establishment, but also with others who caught his eye and lived in the houses of other Tutors.[1]

Dr Hornby had received complaints, most recently from Wolley-Dod, a highly respected senior housemaster. Browning had lately struck up a friendship with a boy called George Nathaniel Curzon, the son of the 4th Baron Scarsdale, who was one of Wolley-Dod's pupils. Hornby had ordered Browning to desist, to limit his contacts to his own boys, and not to act with impropriety. Browning had submitted with a bad grace and, with characteristic folly, had made a point of visiting Curzon and seeing his parents during the holidays.

Hornby had let the matter rest, unable in fact, to do anything else, since Browning had not committed a crime and could not be disciplined without a reason. Suspicion itself was not enough. Sex was a subject that could not be mentioned. Anyway, no one had any proof that Browning's friendships were anything other than platonic eccentricities.

Introducing the dilemma

When, however, he had made the mistake about the pupils, had gone against a known regulation, and had taken a special permission for granted, he had given Hornby the necessary pretext. Hornby had acted without hesitation, and put an end to Browning's employment. All the same, Hornby had erred, not being able, even to his colleagues, to explain the actual reason for having dismissed him.

Browning, too, remained in the dark since no one ever dared to suggest what was obvious to all, that Hornby feared he was a homosexual or, at least, a dangerous paedophile. Forty years after the event he still remained 'entirely ignorant' of the real reason behind the disaster from which, it evolved, there was no appeal.

Angry parents had written to Hornby protesting at having to alter their arrangements. One, Knatchbull-Hugessen, a distinguished Liberal Member of Parliament, even raised the matter in the House of Commons. Browning, himself, had petitioned the Provost. All, it proved, to no avail. Under a recent Act of Parliament which governed the management of endowed schools, the right to engage or dismiss assistants had been committed without appeal into the hands of the schools' headmasters. Therefore Hornby's decision was final. Browning was condemned without redress. For the rest of his life he felt a victim of Dr Hornby's personal spite, and was never able, even for a day, to forget the shock of such a shattering catastrophe.

Behind the scenes in this crisis, as in most events in life, lay the spirit of the times. Ever since the 1830s when the problems of sex at boys' schools had been openly mentioned for the first time – in the *Quarterly Journal of Education*[2] – the fear of immorality and vice had become a matter of growing anxiety.

The problem itself was as old as the hills, but for several special and interesting reasons, by the later decades of the nineteenth century – by the time, therefore, of Browning's dismissal – it had grown to one of national concern. For the places in which this problem arose, the exclusive precincts of public schools, had more than doubled in thirty years. On all sides new colleges like Wellington, Marlborough, Cheltenham,

Haileybury, had been established beside the old foundations of Eton, Harrow, Winchester, Westminster. They supplied a new and increasing demand, the education of the middle classes. Thousands of boys who might previously have stayed at home and enjoyed normal, family lives were now living together like monks. It was only natural in these circumstances that moral problems should come to the surface to a new and unforseen extent, and equally natural that public opinion should demand that the schools should try to tackle them.

At Eton itself, the authoritative view of staff and parents on the general question of sexual immorality was not yet quite so strict as it was in later years to become. Thanks to an aristocratic tradition of urbane tolerance towards moral peccadillos, it still turned a blind eye to many a gentle boyish friendship and many a warm tutorial hug that comforted the hearts of the young and lonely, and at their best were entirely innocent. But clear warnings were in the sky. Only three years before, in April 1872, the admired assistant, William Johnson (who subsequently changed his name to Cory), who epitomised the loving tutor at its best, had been asked, like Browning, suddenly to leave. No one knew the exact reason, but everyone guessed that morals came into it. The cult of games as an antidote to 'vice' was spreading rapidly throughout the school under the athletic Dr Hornby, an Oxford Blue and renowned alpinist. 'Manly' and 'pure' were soon to be catchwords for all that he wished his boys to be. The mere sight of Oscar Browning with his pale face and effeminate manner was enough in itself to make Hornby suspicious.

So although Browning deserved to be sacked, if only for serious indiscretion, he was sacked also, like it or not, because of the moral and social pressures of his times.

His life, of course, had to go on; for he had to earn his own living, being without a private income, and also to care for his mother and a sister. So he retired to King's College, Cambridge, of which he held a Founder's Fellowship, and settled down to tutoring and lecturing. He wished, above all, to redeem his name. He planned to write a *magnum opus*; to become a distinguished professor of history, to train students to become statesmen, to ascend the administrative ladder of King's – possibly even to become the Provost.

All these high ideals were quite within his capability; yet, after thirty years, when he retired at the age of seventy, he was still only an ordinary Fellow, and had no public reputation except as a Cambridge personality. Something had always blocked his progress, the same something that had made Hornby determine, come what might, to sack him.

This was a deeply-held suspicion, felt by all who had to deal with him that, at heart, he was not serious; that self-interest and self-advertisement were, at bottom, his real motives; whether put forward in the name of King's, or in the service of the University. Also, his homosexual leanings did not, of course, pass unnoticed. A permanent court of admiring students led to undesirable comment. Yet, the fact of the matter was that these attachments were mostly innocent. Many boys and their parents, too, wrote him hundreds of letters to prove it.

These letters which he filed carefully, together with others from friends and family, numbering in total many thousands, form a remarkable archive from which the student of human nature may observe a fascinating fellow being. For if a man is known by his friends, so he may be known by their letters; and every facet of Browning's life is lit – sometimes darkened too – by the intimate, personal letters he kept. They reveal his life as an Eton housemaster; his work as a busy don at Cambridge; his family life as a loving son; his secret life as a homosexual. Pieced together like a jig-saw puzzle, they compose a most extra-ordinary picture – that of a man who was almost a genius; a teacher who inspired unusual devotion; a person of super-human energy; a snob of really laughable proportions; a figure of Tweedledum-like girth; an egocentric of limitless capacity.

These conflicting characteristics led him in many opposing directions. His life at Eton was very successful and yet destroyed by his lack of judgement; his work as a don was never fulfilled because of his sloth and social ambition; his career as a teacher was truly inspired but never rewarded because of his vanity; his friendships with men like Oscar Wilde, which followed after his departure from Eton, may have released his imprisoned spirit and may have given him moments of delight, but on several occasions they took him up to the edge of legal catastrophe.

The final judgement is extremely difficult. Had he lived before Victoria in times that were morally less exacting – in, for example, the headmastership of Keate which ended in 1834 – he would not have been rebuked at all. Had he been forgiven by Hornby, and agreed to accept the prevailing conventions, adopted Muscular Christianity, kept his erotic dreams in the background, and curbed his gifts for boyish friendships, he might have learnt his lesson over Curzon, continued to run an excellent house, retired with honour in middle-age, possibly even become Headmaster.

As it was, he lost everything. He had to start his life afresh, and he found in the blander atmosphere of Cambridge more time for idle thoughts, more people with whom to share them, more leisure for social activities, more opportunities for sexual adventure.

So he became a Cambridge character, known to the world as O.B. Every term he did less and less. Every year he got fatter and fatter. In the end he was only remembered for being a man with two initials, which, thanks to one of his admirers, H.B. Ottley, a student of Trinity, formed the subject of a clever joke.[3]

> O, be obedient, great O.B.
> To Nature's stern decrees;
> Or, portly one, as now you are
> You'll soon be too obese.

His portrait hangs in Hall at King's; his bust adorns the Provost's Lodge; his books grace the shelves of the Library; few people ever look at them.

Dr Hornby perhaps was right. Browning did deserve to be sacrificed: not because of his love of youth, but because of his love of himself. In a Christian society, he committed one of its gravest sins: quite apart from failing to be 'pure in heart', at the same time he wasted his precious gifts in triviality.

CHAPTER II

Eton, King's, and Eton

Browning was born in 1837, just in the reign of William IV, on a day famous for its dense fog, the thickest anyone ever remembered, which descended suddenly about noon on Tuesday 17th January. Traffic came to a total halt, many people were lost completely, and Mrs Browning nearly died because of the late appearance of the doctor. She gave birth to twin boys, the elder dying, the younger, Oscar, only surviving thanks to the nurse. He was weak and small, and ever afterwards, attributed his lack of height and health to his sudden and premature arrival.

The registration of births and deaths had not then been put into effect, so that no birth certificate exists, but a neat entry concerning his baptism may still be seen in the parish records.[1] He was safely christened on 8th April in the new, classical St Pancras church by the curate, the Reverend William Arrowsmith who had also buried his little sister, Grace Browning, aged three, before Christmas the previous year.[2] Possibly distress at Grace's loss had been the cause of his mother's near miscarriage.

The Browning family came from Gloucestershire, and were prominent there in the fourteenth century, owning land in the Vale of Berkeley, having originally come from Friesland. Browning's branch had migrated to London, and his great-grandfather, in the eighteenth century, had married an heiress in Westminster Abbey. His father owned a prosperous distillery, and lived in comparative wealth and elegance at No 8, Cumberland Terrace, a graceful house by Regent's Park. He seems, however, to have lost money for shortly after Browning's birth he moved to a smaller house at Windsor. From there he continued to work in London, and Browning recorded in later years his childhood memories of visiting the warehouse, of the ghostly shadows of enormous vats and the crystal streams of scented spirit.

There were two sons and one daughter already in the family, and later on there were two more daughters. Browning remained the youngest boy, but, in spite of having younger sisters, he always kept his place as his mother's favourite. For five years he had been her baby, and for the rest of her life, for fifty-two years, he retained his place as her undisputed darling.

His early education was desultory. He went to various schools and tutors, beginning Latin when he was four, and taking to Greek at the age of eight. His mother was a highly educated woman and, clearly, watched his progress seriously. It was hoped he would go to Eton as a Scholar – both his brothers had been there before him – and after having his name accepted he went to live with the elder, William, to prepare himself for the examination.

William was then curate of Everdon, a delightful parish close to Daventry, the rector of which was George Green, a former assistant master at Eton, who later on became a Fellow. In characteristic Victorian manner, William married his rector's daughter, and a wedding present still survives: a massively bound Family Bible, given to him by Browning and others, bearing Browning's neat signature. With William, Browning was extremely happy, enjoying country life to the full with others boys who were also pupils, and he passed his entrance examination in the summer of the year 1850. He went to Eton the following January, rather older than many new boys, a few days before his fourteenth birthday.

Although improved since the days of Keate when, in the 1820s and 1830s the boys had ruled their own lives and only seen the staff in the classrooms, Eton at that time was still a rough world of its own in which the weaker boys were helpless, and where the delights and depravities of vice were imposed on the youngest without restraint. Like most new boys, Browning was innocent, knowing only a family circle of loving parents, brothers and sisters. Although he only hints in his memoirs at the harsh brutalities of life in College, of the bestialities of Long Chamber, the great mediaeval open dormitory, the whole experience obviously shocked him. As to what he discovered of sex, what he was made to endure, one cannot, of course, be precise since he was unable to describe it. That he was clearly ashamed, repelled and disgusted, is made evident by his nephew, Wortham, who knew him well, and who wrote his life with access to his private papers.

Small, shy and unathletic, he was not happy in his first years, the more so doubtless for being a 'Tug'. This was the slang name given to Scholars who, under the Founder's Statutes, were forced to wear a woollen gown, making them undesirably conspicuous and setting them apart as socially inferior. He often suffered from imagined insults, and complained of the wickedness of unknown enemies, clear beginnings of a later complex. His work, however, progressed favourably, and his tutor, the gentle William Johnson, wrote the following report at the end of the year.

> Unlike many Collegers who work in an Utilitarian spirit and value their classics only for the sake of success in trials, Oscar reads like a student of literature, sympathises with me and goes along with me in the pursuit of what is beautiful in poetry or elsewhere and, one may say, makes literary alliances more or less durable with boys of the gentler mould. So here at last I have found a genuine student combining taste with knowledge, aesthetics with grammar, sociability with thoughtfulness . . .[3]

Johnson's letter is only a fragment, addressed to someone who is not specified, most probably Browning's mother. Whoever it was, Browning got hold of it, and wrote on the bottom in pious gratitude, 'and may God in his mercy grant that I may not disappoint him'.

In his sixteenth year he began a journal, perhaps because of the loss of his father, and therefore of someone in whom to confide, who had died suddenly on Easter day. Although now unfortunately lost, it was used by Wortham in his biography and shows clearly his state of mind as he strove to maintain the shifting balance between his ambitions and his capabilities, and struggled to understand himself. His growing personal sexual awareness whose demands excited as well as revolted him can be seen, as can his profound desire for someone to love, his schoolboy longing to be a Napoleon, and his equal resolve to obtain immortality by brilliant poetic or literary achievement. Even towards the end of his time when he moved away from Long Chamber, gained greater freedom and privacy, and found friendship in the homely quarters of the newly appointed Master in College, he was never really happy at Eton. As the years passed his promise faded, sloth began to get the better of him (the first stirrings of his life's enemy) and even his admirer, William Johnson, began to give him critical reports.

These must have really upset him, as Johnson had taught him all he knew, given him a genuine love of the classics, developed his passion for English literature, enabled him to study French and Italian, encouraged his interest in music and the arts, and even instructed him in mathematics, a subject he always found objectionable. Most of all, Johnson had opened the boy's eyes to the aims and skills of teaching itself. No amount of dispute with Johnson after returning to Eton as a master ever dimmed his love for his tutor or reduced his opinion of the latter's genius. To have failed him after so much encouragement, the one person in the whole of Eton who really seemed to have understood him, must have been a serious blow.

Browning had one scholastic triumph. In the summer of 1854 he entered and won a competition to compose and orate a formal address to Queen Victoria and the Prince Consort. The Queen, as it happened, failed to arrive, but the Prince came with two of his sons, the Prince of Wales and Prince Alfred, both dressed in Highland costume, accompanied also by the King of Portugal with his brother, the Duke of Oporto. Arrayed in traditional Speech Day dress of a tail coat and knee breeches, silk stockings and black pumps, Browning chose for his subject the Russian retreat in the Crimean war, and declaimed before the assembled school how,

> Now that sweet Peace hath spread her silver wings
> And fled affrighted from the strife of Kings –
> With heartfelt joy thy Presence here we see,
> And hail security and Peace in thee![4]

The performance lasted for five minutes, the poem containing seventy lines. The Prince Consort appeared to be pleased, and gave the blushing scholar a hearty handshake.

Never a popular boy, he was also, rather unexpectedly, made a member of the Eton Society, commonly known as 'Pop'. It was then a serious debating society, and election to it was an academic honour for which he had every reason to be proud.

When he left in 1856, by then aged nineteen, although he had never been a star performer – he was only fourth in the school in seniority, and always perfectly hopeless at games – he was more confident of making his mark and more at ease in society at large than many of his more successful friends. He had started to mix with distinguished people, members of the Bar and politicians; he had travelled abroad with his mother and sisters who had left Windsor on his father's death and moved to a house in the centre of Brussels; he had even accompanied the King of the Belgians as an honorary member of the royal suite, when the latter paid a visit to Calais to meet the Emperor and Empress of France. This was a special treat for a schoolboy, but in Browning's case it was also evidence of his lifelong passion for nobility and royalty.

The company of women never appealed to him. Unlike many adolescent diarists, he never painted idealised portraits of the flowerlike beauties of early sweethearts. He wrote only of secret passions for other boys he knew at Eton, sometimes boys he had never spoken to, passing Davids he had only seen. One such was called Dunmore whom he loved with a pure embracing warmth that was fanned to an almost unbearable heat by the chance discovery, sometime later, that the boy was also a wealthy nobleman.

His real loves in these years – before he went to university and before he developed his natural ability for making generous and lasting friendships – were reading history and listening to music. Both these, like meeting the great, remained enduring passions. He was not a good musician himself since he could never do anything well with his hands, and his sense of pitch was always dreadful. He sang boisterously nevertheless, and played the

piano with cheerful enthusiasm. As to books, he read vora-
ciously, as a list of volumes in his room at Eton testifies.

In the summer of 1856, after enduring weeks of uncertainty,
he was offered the vital vacancy at King's, the sister foundation
to Eton at Cambridge, to which Scholars could go by right so
long as they passed the examination and had not reached the
age of twenty. He left Eton without regret, giving and receiving
the quantities of books that custom demanded of friends (a
tradition that was soon to be succeeded by the cheaper, recipro-
cal exchange of photographs) and having his gown 'ripped' by
the Provost, another quaint, mediaeval ceremony that was also
to vanish soon.

He faced the future now with confidence, for once at King's,
his career was assured. He would take his degree as a matter of
right, under another ancient practice that was just about to be
swept away, and automatically become a Fellow. In spite of a
poor final report from Johnson, he spent a happy summer
holiday, travelling abroad with his mother and family, proudly
aware of approaching manhood, thankful at last to have left his
schooldays behind.

Browning's four years at Cambridge were spent in a cheerfully
normal fashion, undisturbed by the personal conflicts that
always seemed to surround him afterwards. He simply enjoyed
the perennial delights of every ordinary undergraduate: the
exquisite beauty of Cambridge itself, its green lawns and noble
courts; boating, walking, riding, swimming; hearty breakfasts,
jovial teaparties; the pleasures of conversation and friendship.

At King's he was thought to be rather a prig – he was
somewhat aloof and independent – but as all Kingsmen were
Old Etonians, forming a select and exclusive group from which
he always wished to escape, he did not expect to be very
popular.

Except for Frank Warre Cornish who followed him there a
year afterwards and to whom he remained attached for life, all
his friends came from other colleges. Outside King's he found
men, particularly those who came from Trinity such as Henry
Sidgwick and George Trevelyan, who made him feel he was

likeable and normal, who thought him both amusing and intelligent. Many had been at school at Rugby, and brought with them the high seriousness that was Dr Arnold's finest legacy. They shared Browning's radical views, his deep and simple religious convictions, his concern at the narrowness of education, his dislike of the growing cult of athleticism; all opinions of his which were to strengthen over the years.

He was soon invited to join the 'Apostles', the long-established coterie of friends which met to discuss intellectual topics. He also joined the Cambridge Union, and became its President in 1859, the first from King's for nineteen years.

He became a Fellow in 1859, described in the quaint manner of the College's *Liber Protocol*, as Oscar Browning, a learned youth. He was unable to attend the actual ceremony, being in bed with scarlet fever. A year later he took his degree, not expecting high distinction, being as he said 'a notorious polymath', always darting from subject to subject, but he came fourth in the Classical Tripos. This was a better result than at first appeared as the three above him were bracketed first.

His real ambition was to travel, to study the governments of other countries, then to read at the English Bar and finally to return to the University to teach history and political science. Instead, by chance, he returned to Eton. It had long been the custom for assistant masters to be drawn only from graduates of King's, thus to be always Old Etonians. This practice was naturally often criticised and was soon, in fact, to be abolished. Unexpectedly receiving a telegram from Dr Goodford, the school's Headmaster, offering him a post the following summer, he had little difficulty in deciding to accept it.

The position carried a handsome salary, far greater than that of his Fellowship, and gave him the chance at little expense, to provide a home for his mother and sisters. As to his plans to become a teacher, he could do that just as well at Eton, indeed, possibly even better, knowing well the transcendent importance of training children at an early age to work hard and think seriously, to question decisions as well as accept them. Also, he might promote reforms, and put an end to some of the abuses, especially the prevalence of homosexuality which had so disgusted him when in College.

If he failed, he had an alternative. He could always return to King's, having as he did a Fellowship for life, and there pursue his original plans to teach at the University.

CHAPTER III

In loco parentis

In the 1860s as Oscar Browning returned to Eton, it so happened that several of the country's oldest schools, Eton first among them, were made the subject of a Parliamentary Inquiry. Thus we are lucky to have a detailed picture of the school at this important moment in his life, the product of oral and written evidence of the Fellows, masters, pupils and parents, as well as submissions from Browning himself. It stands before us, sharply delineated, a little secluded world of its own, a place of barbarous freedoms and delights, still enjoying a pastoral tranquillity, where boys swam naked in the Thames, and a free morning could be passed in fishing. '. . . a good lot of trouts in the river . . .' wrote Alexander Clark-Kennedy to his father and mother who lived in Scotland.

In Browning's time the ancient College, founded in the year 1440, was still governed much as it had been during the Middle Ages. This, in fact, was the cause of the Inquiry: with other schools like Winchester, securely bound in their Founders' Statutes, it had failed completely to move with the times, and was still teaching by the same methods the same extremely limited curriculum as it had peacefully for four centuries.

The education was entirely classical, the method, the ancient one of repetition; and the books used, like the Eton Grammars, full of mistakes and almost useless. The Greek Grammar was written in Latin so that only scholars could understand it. Mathematics was only taught for three obligatory periods per week, and anything else like science or history, modern geography or European languages were only provided as voluntary extras. The authorities thought them a waste of time, and most of the parents heartily shared their prejudices.

Formal lessons were held in the classroom, the classes being known as Divisions, containing sometimes one hundred boys whom no master could possibly control, even with frequent threats of the birch. Browning had eighty boys in his Division when he returned to Eton in 1860, 'many of them very unruly'. The youngest was eleven, the eldest sixteen. In these Divisions the master's task was not to teach but only to examine. He would hear work previously set – so many lines of Latin or Greek – and then, as the period came to a close, set some more for the following period. Every boy was supposed to prepare them, but only a handful ever did so. The majority relied on not being asked, or doing their best with a crib if they happened to be called for. This part of the work was onerous and unproductive for the great majority; only a few at the top of the school ever took their classwork seriously. In complete contrast, that part held in a master's study or 'pupil-room', was often varied and extremely good.

Every boy had to have a 'tutor', that is to say a classical assistant, usually in fact the boy's housemaster, with whom he remained throughout his schooldays. With him he established a close relationship. In the phrase of the time, he 'loved his tutor'. Often the lonely boy whose parents, perhaps, were away in India, not to return for years and years, came to regard his tutor with real affection.

In these informal sessions in pupil-room the boy was supposed to prepare his classwork under his tutor's friendly guidance; but if the tutor was a man of ability as Johnson had been in Browning's case, and as Browning was to a high degree, the official work became almost a sideline. Every kind of subject was discussed: philosophy, history, literature, the arts; any idea that sprang to mind from the texts which the boys were working to prepare. The Eton system, widely criticised and soon to be greatly changed after the report of the Commission of Inquiry, could in the hands of a gifted teacher, provide a boy with a better education than anything contained in a fixed and limited curriculum.

Still, the classwork had to be done, whatever the delight of other subjects, and for every master and every boy it remained a paramount obligation. In Browning's first year as a master, 1860–1861, his pupils in Division studied the following, most of which as well as translating, they had to commit to unwilling memory:

432 Lines	Farnaby Epigrams	Eton Edition
964 Lines	Aesop's Fables	Eton Edition
720 Lines	Ovid Selections	Eton Edition
650 Lines	Ovid Metamorphoses	Eton Edition
660 Lines	Caesar	Eton Edition
20 Chapters	Greek Testament	Oxford Text

Browning stated in written evidence that in every week with forty pupils (those boys to whom he was tutor), taking them separately in groups of ten, he spent six hours every day, usually seven days per week, teaching and hearing all these tedious exercises. All in all he worked very hard, from six in the morning until twelve at night. During the term or 'half' as it was called (from days gone by when travel was difficult and the boys had only two holidays) there was little time for leisure or recreation.

There were, however, compensations. He earned an excellent income at Eton, as well as the usual long vacations. During these, apart from resting, Browning and many other assistants assumed the classic role of the paedagogue and conducted boys about the Continent for which they received a handsome fee including, of course, a free holiday.

His basic salary was only nominal, a mere forty guineas per annum for the routine work of teaching in the classroom. To this he added fees for pupils (the number of pupils was limited to forty) at ten to twenty guineas a year each, according to the wealth of the pupils' parents. Once he got a house in 1862, also limited to forty boys, he was able to live without anxiety. The average charge for each boy was about ninety guineas per annum for supposedly furnished lodging and board. Out of this, according to general consent, about fifty pounds at the end of the year could be put in the bank by the master as absolute profit.

Thus, with a house of forty boys, an annual income could look like this:

In loco parentis

Annual salary	40 gns	£ 42
40 boarders at	90 gns	£ 3780
20 pupils at	10 gns	£ 210
20 pupils at	20 gns	£ 420
10 pupils' leaving presents at	£15	£ 150
		£ 4602
Deduct 50% of Boarders' fees for expenses		£ 1890
Net annual profit		£ 2712

Browning's house to begin with was small, in fact the smallest in the school, containing only nine boarders, together with his mother and his two sisters. They made it very cosy, however. It was not long before it gained a reputation for being something out of the ordinary, more liberal and more homelike than the usual run of school boarding houses. Prospective parents began to write to him.

An Admiral Drew asked for advice. His boy was down for Browning's house but he would have preferred him to become a Colleger, that is to say, to take a scholarship. He was worried, however, about his Latin. He was only eight and doing very well at Mrs Hibburd's academy at Clewer but the trouble was, his teacher was a woman, and 'Ladies Latin', he opined dogmatically, 'is not always of the best quality'.

A Mr Hunt asked for reservations. He wanted his boys, aged eight and ten, to come to Browning's in two years' time. In fact they did so in 1870, forcefully removed from their school at Brighton 'on account of their being so terribly coddled'.

The aristocracy also wrote, rather haughtily in the third person, like Lady Southdown in *Vanity Fair*.

Lady Isabella Schuster presents her compliments to Mr Oscar Browning and both she and Mr Schuster are anxious to have their only son placed in his house (having heard such a good report of him through Mr Magniac). Lady Isabella's boy, William Somers Leo Schuster will be 10 years old on 22nd September and Mr and Lady Isabella would like him to enter Mr Browning's house in *2*

23

years time and Lady Isabella hopes by writing *now* that Mr Oscar Browning may then have a vacant place for their son. Mr & Lady Isabella Schuster would be glad to learn Mr Oscar Browning's terms.[1]

Other letters came, naturally, from the parents of boys already in the house. Thus Lady Caroline Turnor, who married a commoner like Lady Isabella, presented her compliments to Mr Browning and would, she said, feel greatly obliged if news could be sent of her son, Herbert, who she believed had not been well. Browning seems to have risen to this, and replied that Herbert was merely malingering. His letters to parents were often sharp. Lady Caroline appears to have nettled him. Little Herbert was made to repent and to pen a submissive confession to his father who immediately sent it back to Browning. 'I hope you will allow me to forgive him', he requested nervously.

An early boarder was Charlie Murray, the son of Sir Charles Murray the diplomatist, for whose sake Queen Victoria had actually declared war on Persia to refute a charge of 'odious offences'. The kind of parent Browning liked, he was well-to-do and aristocratic, the son of the 5th Earl of Dunmore. An eccentric, dominant and loving father, he wrote about his son ceaselessly, sometimes as often as twice a week, wasting much of Browning's time. His long letters are really interesting, revealing as much about himself as they do about contemporary attitudes. Some parents rather grovelled, but Sir Charles was positively dictatorial.

He wrote first in 1863, after Charlie's first half, saying that Charlie looked well which, he said, was evident proof of the healthy sufficiency of Browning's 'board'. Browning always spent a lot on catering, a cause of annoyance to many of his colleagues who were forced to do the same to keep up with him. Charlie himself had been very happy, and reported that everything was 'awfully jolly'.

The next letter, a fortnight later in January 1864, touched on an oft recurring theme, one that a century of civilisation has failed to remove from parental agenda. Charlie kept his hands in his pockets, and nothing on earth could make him remove them. Sir Charles wrote from the Dresden legation:[2]

> On the whole we are very well satisfied with his conduct & manners but there are one or two points to which I wish to direct yr attention. When he returned we found that he had acquired an abominable habit of *always* keeping his hands in his trowser pockets; finding that all observations on the subject were unavailing and observing that the said pockets were generally receptacles for peas, pebbles & all kinds of rubbish, I had the pockets cut out of all his trowsers & the side apertures sewed up: I beg now for the future that whenever he has any trowsers made at Eton you will instruct the tailor to make them without pockets . . . We find also that he has got a bad habit of eating a great deal too fast & also of lolling & leaning back on his chair at meals – these we have endeavoured to correct, & if you observe anything of the kind I hope you will do so too – there are few things that distinguish a gentleman from a snob more than the manner in which he comes into a room & sits at table – hence my war on the trowser pockets & on the lolling in his chair; he is a very merry, amiable & affectionate boy & I trust that the thoughtlessness of which we now complain will disappear with his advancing years.

Another continuing problem with Charlie, equally familiar to modern parents, was the writing of the weekly letter. Performance here got worse and worse until, by April the following year, in the face of increasing parental annoyance, Charlie began to resort to deceit. Having written three letters at the same time, each bearing different dates, he unwisely posted them simultaneously. Of course, they all arrived together. To explain this rather strange coincidence he told his extremely suspicious parent that the first and second must have been lost – perhaps by the servant to whom he had given them – and then despatched quite by chance by the same post as the third and last. Twenty years of professional diplomacy including five at the court of Persia had taught Sir Charles to be very sceptical, and once Charlie came back for the holidays he took him aside, as he wrote to Browning, and sternly made him confess to the obvious truth.

25

In loco parentis

Sir Charles was then *en poste* in Saxony which entitled Charlie to a week's travelling on top of the appointed length of the holidays, but Sir Charles made him return on time as a final reminder not to lie. Browning was asked to stop his pocket money – two shillings and six pence per week – until he had received from his own hand Charlie's weekly letter to his parent.

Then, left alone in the residence, suddenly empty of Charlie's laughter, Sir Charles was filled with sorrow and remorse, and wrote to Browning an apologia, explaining Charlie's lonely upbringing and the probable effect it had made on his character.

> It must not be forgotten in his case that he lost his mother before he was 10 days old, & my aunt who brought him up being a great invalid he was necessarily during the early years of his childhood left almost entirely in the charge of nursery governesses & maids; and these, I am sorry to say, however *respectable* & highly recommended they may be, generally excuse themselves from blame by untruth or evasion . . .

Browning showed these letters to his mother whose job it was to give out the allowances – whose important task it had been, too, to attend to Charlie's trouser pockets. Neither threats nor cajolery prevailed. (Could it have been that without pockets Charlie had nowhere to keep his pocket money and determined therefore to do without it?) Again he failed to write to his father, and again his father wrote to Browning.

> If I knew of any good strict tutor to whom I could send him to work hard during his summer holidays instead of amusing himself in Scotland or on the Continent, I would avail myself of the opportunity without hesitation . . . I have often noticed that nervous, frightened manner that he has when questioned upon any subject connected with his conduct, he has had it from childhood . . . I have remarked in the boy from his early childhood, strangely mixed with that nervous timidity of manner which you have observed, a most determined obstinacy . . .

In loco parentis

Browning disliked the idea of a tutor and told Sir Charles that he did not agree with it. He thought Charlie would be much better 'with an autumn of vigorous exercise in Scotland'. Faced with the threat of imprisonment in August, Charlie quickly wrote and repented. His father was pleased but refused to give in. 'What have you done about Charlie's holidays, time presses?' he telegraphed to Browning on July 30th. The half ended on August 4th. Browning was left without any choice. He sent Charlie to a Mr Charles who lived at Friskney on the coast of Lincolnshire. He, himself, went to 'Chamouni'. 'My chief motive for Alpine travel was health', he wrote, 'and as to its beneficial results in that respect there can be no doubt. I could not have got through my work at Eton without it.'

Browning returned to Eton refreshed, to find a brace of grouse from Sir Charles, and a further, long admonitory letter.

Whether Browning got tired of Charlie, or whether he found Charlie's conduct as bad as appears from the following letters, in the middle of the half the next summer, June 1866, he gave him such a bad report that Sir Charles decided to take him away.

Charlie was then extremely distressed. For once, he wrote to his father in haste.

July 7th [1866]

Dear Papa,

I can not tell you how sorry I was to hear that you are going to take me away this half. Is it not possible, dear Papa, for me to stay a little longer here and try to retrieve my character. Mr Browning says that he is quite willing to keep me if you let me stay, and I am *sure*, dear Papa, that I am much better than I have been for some time, and though I have got worse it is because I am up to a very hard master and I have *told the truth* what for the last year I should have got out of with a lie or a shuffle I have this half borne the punishment of and on my honour I have not told an untruth in schoolwork this half. I cannot tell you how hard it has been to stop myself, but I have, and though I acknowledge that I have been very idle, I have been straightforward. Dear Papa, this has been a very dreadful warning and if you let me stay I assure you it will not be lost on me, just try me one more half and I will do you and myself honour.

I remain, dear Papa, Your very affte son, C.J. Murray

Charlie's letter was sent to Browning (hence its survival amongst his papers) and Browning decided to let him stay. He wrote to Sir Charles to advise him accordingly. Sir Charles was perfectly ready to relent, and once the following half had begun he reported to Browning about the tasks of the holidays.

Copenhagen
September 26th

My dear Sir

I did not answer yr letter from Switzerland while you were rambling among the Alps – knowing how unpalateable all correspondence & especially letters relating to 'shop' must be at such a time. Charlie has remained with us all the holidays & I must do him the justice to say that he has conducted himself very well – I cannot say that we have been able to extract from him any of that zeal or ardour in the pursuit of knowledge which alone can lead to future excellence – but how few boys possess it: on the other hand he has been very docile and willing to go through the light tasks we have imposed upon him. I have taken him through the 3 first books of the Iliad . . . also the 3rd and 4th Books of the Aeneid & the 3rd B of Horace's Odes . . . With my wife he has daily read some French or German with a sprinkling of Natural History . . . Tho'a strong well-grown boy I do not think that his *stomach* is a strong one, & unfortunately he taxes it's powers most unnecessarily by eating a great deal too fast! I wish he could be cured of this habit – & if you observe it at table pray try & check it – for not even a strong stomach can bear without injury the habitual infliction of unmasticated food.

I do hope & trust that the improvement which you have noticed and reported will continue [he wrote again a month later]. With *us* I must say that during last holidays he was very docile and amiable & the only thing I found fault with was his lack of *energy* in everything & his too great tendency to lounge & loll on sofas & armchairs – these trifles betoken character – Goethe never had an armchair till he was 74 & my wife's mother has never had one to this day!

In loco parentis

Thus Sir Charles's letters continued, full of affection and individuality, liberally sprinkled with direct commands which Browning usually managed to ignore. Charlie at last began to do better, and left in 1868 to follow his father into diplomacy. Browning kept in touch with the family and later on stayed with Sir Charles when the latter became the ambassador to Portugal. Many threads in the social network connected the busy outside world to the microcosmic world of the Eton housemaster.

Another valuable parental contact which Browning made in these years was with the celebrated sculptor, William Story.

Browning met him in 1862, visiting Rome where the latter lived, and the two immediately formed a productive friendship. Thanks to an introduction from Story he met his namesake, Robert Browning, with whom, later, he was often confused when he himself attained celebrity; and he met, too, at different times, many other literary lions like Motley, Trollope, Longfellow and Thackeray. He often stayed with the Storys in Rome, and as, like many American expatriates enjoying Europe in that era, they were both rich and extremely sociable, he saw at their house almost everybody who rose to the surface of Roman Society: the princes, cardinals, ambassadors and generals that all his life he loved to collect.

The Storys had two beloved sons who went to Eton in 1865, both as boarders in Browning's house, and, in a very American manner, they worried about them both continually. They wrote to Browning and his mother at length, and when upset they wrote repeatedly, both at the same time, even using the same expressions, appealing to mother and son simultaneously in what must have felt like a perfect bombardment.

The boys were evidently happy, clearly feeling the joy of escape from their too protective and fussy parents. Soon, however, they got into trouble, not because they were ever wicked but simply because they were thoroughly American and unaware of English traditions, especially those embodied in Eton. Their father's first letter to Browning painfully reveals their parents' distress at the unexpected results of their ignorance.

In loco parentis

'My dear Browning,' Story wrote on the 10th December 1868,[3]

> your reports of my boys were in every respect far from gratifying – but I confess that we were all very very much pained and shocked by the statement that 'Waldo had received a flogging because he had allowed Julian to write out a punishment.' I had supposed that this barbarous system of flogging was abandoned except in cases where it was necessary as a dernier resort . . . But here is a boy scarcely six weeks at school for the first time, ignorant of its usages and strict requirements, who for a first offence is flogged and disgraced in his own eyes & in the eyes of his school-mates. The first time he comes face to face with the head master, that person flogs him . . . It is the first blow he ever received as a punishment. We have all felt it very much, & I do not think it has been out of our minds a quarter of an hour since we heard it.

Many of the letters in Browning's collection disclose the fact that at some moment he unexpectedly wrote to parents, or worse still, summoned them to Eton, to say that their sons were not doing well, had poor marks or bad companions, and ought perhaps to be taken away. His motive, normally, was quite straightforward. He wished to give the parents a shock which they in turn would pass on to their sons to make them abandon their wayward habits. The tactic usually worked to perfection. Distracted parents begged for a reprieve, and the erring scholars implored forgiveness. How well it came off has already been seen in the correspondence with Sir Charles Murray.

At times, however, the case was different. Browning used to tire of boys when they reached the age of sexual maturity: boys previously spoilt or favoured, often ones who were charming and clever, sometimes those he had taken abroad – with, of course, parental consent – on long cultural tours in the holidays. Then he used to write to the parents the same letter of complaint and warning with, however, a different motive. Suddenly hating the fallen favourites, he only wanted to wound and punish them. The boys' parents were naturally astounded, only recently having been told that their sons were enjoying

Browning's approval. The boys, too, were baffled and hurt. In these cases, it has to be said, that Browning behaved with malice, and most dishonourably.

In the summer of 1871, he did this suddenly to Waldo and Julian. He had spent the Easter holidays in Rome, and having, it seems, got tired of the boys, for what reason cannot be ascertained, he injudiciously gossiped about them. Of course, what he said got back to the parents, and later on when back at Eton, he received an outraged letter from the father.

Since leaving Rome I have heard on my journey from no less than four entirely separate persons that you have vilified both my boys & especially Waldo to them in so strong & severe terms, that they deemed it their duty to report this to me. You have said they were bad boys without morals & with no regard to truth – liars is the word you used – you said more too – & not content with this you expressed wonder at the mode in which we had brought them up – said they were not only ignorant but bad. You also said that Waldo led away other boys in yr school, & particularly Homfreys – while you said to me that Homfreys you feared had led Waldo away. Now, so long as you talked to me privately about the boys and indicated yr suspicions which you well remember were purely suspicions, based upon no facts except a letter written to Waldo which you opened and never showed me – & which he never saw & which as I now know was the only letter ever written to him by that boy – you were quite right – but when you, their Tutor, go about Europe and vilify them to chance acquaintances you meet on the road, and strive to set their relatives agst them by calling them bad immoral boys, liars and ignoramuses, I think you are passing all bounds of propriety & even of decency. You are secretly endeavoring to blast their good name & repute, while pretending to be their friend. While you say to Mr Homfrey that Waldo is a bad boy who leads his son astray, you say to me directly the contrary . . . My advice to you is not to talk agst the boys in yr house behind their backs.
Yrs Truly, W.W. Story.

No one could guess from Browning's *Memories* in which he writes of the Storys warmly, that really their friendship had ended like this. Their Roman apartment was his 'second home' and, ever ready to mention the famous, he told the world how well he knew them. Waldo was taken away from Eton, and Julian moved to another house. Browning dismissed the matter lightly. If Story chose to behave hysterically there was nothing he – Browning – could really do about it.

The clearest example of Browning's treatment of fallen idols happened in 1864 and concerned a boy called Charlie Palairet. Browning had taken him off to Paris as a special reward for excellent work and also, it seems, in preparation for his early appointment as Captain of the House. During the visit, something went wrong. Possibly Browning was too affectionate. It was Browning's habit on these excursions to enlighten the boys on the subject of sex, to warn of the dangers of masturbation, and to quote its alleged terrible effects: infertility or even madness.[4] Perhaps with Charlie he went too far; maybe Charlie was easily shocked. Boys then, even at school, sometimes almost to the age of twenty, remained in a state of total and amazing innocence.

In view of his subsequent accusation that Charlie was hiding improper literature, a sexual rebuff seems a possibility. However it was, once they returned, and once the Easter half had begun, Browning wrote his accustomed letter, saying that Charlie's conduct was bad and that, perhaps, he ought to be removed. Charlie's parent – apparently his stepmother who also seems to have been a widow (Browning favoured fatherless boys as he found them usually easier to deal with) – wrote back most indignantly.

> I really cannot see from your letters any reason at all why my step son should be moved from Eton, and I do not feel the least inclination to take him away for the next year – the change for the worse which has taken place in him has been so surprisingly sudden that I would fain hope you must be mistaken in your bad opinion of him, unless you were mistaken before – for I received a most unusually good character of Charlie from you – you stated that owing to the very high opinion you entertained of him, you

wished to show him some particular mark of favor, and begged me to allow him to accompany you to Paris for part of the Christmas vacation. He no sooner returns to Eton in January, than your opinion of him undergoes an extraordinary change, and in less than six weeks time nothing can be more unfavorable than your account of him – strange indeed it appears to me that such a quick change can have taken place from the very highest standard of good conduct to almost the lowest degree of *bad*, and for all these reasons I am sure it is very much better that he should not return to your House after Easter . . .[5]

Browning's response is not to hand, it can only be assumed that, as with the Storys, he proceeded without a tremor of guilt to put all the blame on the luckless, rejected loved one.

Of course, there were other times again, when boys really did go wrong, and Browning had to summon their parents to warn them frankly, face to face, that their sons were close to dismissal. The depth of parental shame and grief when such a disaster actually happened shows in their letters with painful clarity. Always they sought to blame themselves, little supposing how their grandchildren, with judgement altered by psychoanalysis and twentieth-century historical criticism, would see them merely as hapless victims of their time.

An early case was that of Augustine Whiteway. In the summer of 1863, Browning lost patience with his conduct, and asked his father to come and see him. Augustine, he said, was being idle; he had broken bounds to go racing at Ascot – two crimes rolled into one. Worst of all he had begun to exhibit all the well-known signs of 'vice' – the languid manner, the nervous flush, the adoption of boys younger than himself in girlish, dreamy, unhealthy friendships.

At the end of the half, he returned to his parents. Shortly afterwards his father wrote:

> Coliford, Bath
> September 2nd 1863

My dear Mr Browning,
    I am very glad to have received your kind note this morn: as it

gives me opportunity to write to you on a subject which has so much engrossed me of late.

I am quite sure that *real kindness* & conscientious duty dictated your entire conduct, in the late very painful interview I had with you about my dear boy.

He has been, for now just five weeks, the constant companion of his dear mother & myself . . . I feel *confident* that he would never knowingly induce a little boy to transgress; but would advise him to the contrary: that he is wholly free from the habits which, it appears, his reserved manner & rumours about him inclined you to suspect.

He freely confesses to his idleness last half, & accounts for it, as being the summer half, & from his having so recently passed 'swimming'.

He has been working, of his own accord, *most industriously* since he has been home . . .

Thus I trust, his intentions for the future are manifest, & that you will yet find him a boy in whom you can place every confidence. I firmly believe he will yet be moulded to your will, and that your past anxiety for him will be repaid by steady & satisfactory improvement.

Believe me, very sincerely yrs, R.H. Whiteway

Augustine, however, was not to be moulded. The next half he ran away. His father wrote distractedly to Browning.[6]

Distressing tidings have reached us to the effect that our (to us still very dear though) unhappy boy has succeeded in taking ship for America, en route for Canada or its borders.

Every effort has been employed to stay his course, but he could no where be found.

A few lines from himself off the coast of Ireland have merely certified to us the fact of his actual departure.

His grieving mother & I can only now stay ourselves in the assurance that 'the Lord reigneth'.

I believe that the fear of me has been the main cause of his unhappy conduct, & which his reserved disposition has brooded over in secret ever since I first wrote to him in a threatening strain.

I desire to take this blame to myself. His conduct at Eton presents the most perfect contrast to my mind to his behaviour at home, which I can only put down to undue restraint here & the utter want of control of himself in the vortex of other scenes.

We will still trust, that the 'fiery trial' that undoubtedly awaits him, will be the affliction in God's Hands to bring him to a right mind & to purify him.

Please offer kind regards from sorrowing Parents to Mrs Browning & Your Sisters – & accept the same for yourself.

Again, regretting the sorrow which has come to you in this matter.

Believe me to be, very sincerely yours, R. Hayman Whiteway

An interesting minor aspect of the drama, concerning Eton's internal discipline, is found in a short note addressed to Browning from Dr Balston, the school's Headmaster, in which it appears that Augustine's father had asked that his son should not be flogged. This was before Augustine's departure, and perhaps hints at the cause of it. The offence appears to have been deception, in giving a false name to tradesmen. Also, however, in another note, the dreaded word 'debaucheries' appears. Whatever the crime, punishment was due, and Dr Balston made it clear that in this matter, the rule was inflexible. 'I feel it my duty to say', he wrote, 'that if his son does not submit . . . I must dismiss him from the school.'

It has to be noted that Augustine's parents never attached any blame to Browning. In fact, they had nothing but admiration for the way in which he had tried to help them. The same was true with most of the parents, whether their sons were upright or wicked. Even those whose sons had left, even for instance Augustine's father, continued to write and ask advice.

A further example was Rose Carden, a clergyman's widow whose second son Browning sacked on his own authority for possessing a pornographic book and for writing a suggestive letter to a friend.

In the summer of 1868 Browning found a prohibited pamphlet – one longs to know its actual title – hidden somewhere in the boy's room which he sent at once to the culprit's mother. She wrote by return to acknowledge its arrival and to offer her own, distraught apologies.

In loco parentis

Endon
Pershore, Worcestershire
May 5th 1868

Dear Mr Browning,

I *cannot tell you* how shocked and grieved I am at Arthur's misconduct.

That a boy brought up in a home in which I can with truth say he has never from his own family heard even a word of impurity – in which he has always been taught from his very childhood by precept *and* example to reverence virtue & goodness; – when I remember that I have guarded him from evil as far as a mother can – by even preventing his associating with any boys in the neighbourhood whom I had reason to think might be objectionable companions for him; – when I think of all this & feel how powerless it has all been to keep him from associating with the evil and the bad and sharing in their wickedness – as the possession of those dreadful papers shows him to have done – I am filled with perplexity and distress. I *could not* look at them myself, but I gave them in their sealed envelope to my Father, with a request that he would open and read them. He did so – said that they were perfectly dreadful – that the Publisher ought to be prosecuted – and immediately threw them into the fire . . .

Painful and grievous as it all is to me I *am glad* that the dreadful papers were found and that Arthur has been exposed and punished: I feel the disgrace of it keenly, for no doubt it is known to the whole school – but I think it may be the means of arresting him in that *facile downward course* on which I grieve to think he has taken the first step . . . I am quite sure that in your conduct to him you will be guided by the best motives, and even though it entailed the grievous necessity of removing him from Eton I should have entire confidence in the justice and rectitude which led you to the decision.

Believe me, Yrs very truly, Rose E. Carden

At the end of the half, Arthur was sacked, not only because of the sinful book but also because, later on, Browning intercepted a letter, written to a boy called David Fullerton, in which Arthur jokingly warned him (referring, presumably, to self-abuse) to be careful 'not to over do it'.

In loco parentis

Browning decided, probably rightly according to the code of
the times, that Arthur's conduct could not be tolerated. Therefore he wrote to Mrs Carden. Although, of course, she was
deeply upset, she never for an instant felt aggrieved, and only
begged for Browning's advice.[7]

September 8th 1868

Dear Mr Browning,
    I cannot complain of – however much I may regret – your
decision with regard to Arthur.
    He has himself – and himself only – to thank for the disgrace he
has incurred and the pain he has inflicted upon me . . .
    Thank you for kindly offering to help me with regard to his
future. I am quite at a loss to know what to do for the best . . .
Would it be well for me to send him to any other Public School?
Harrow for instance . . . ? He has so entirely frustrated all my plans
for him . . .
    Of course with your experience of boys generally and your
knowledge of Arthur's character, your opinion as to my best course
will be very valuable to me. I hope please God that after all he may
turn out a good and upright man, but his conduct gives me many
an anxious hour, and to believe that 'whatever is, is best' is
philosophy which it is sometimes very hard to practise.
    Believe me, Yrs very truly, Rose E. Carden

    In spite of these distressing interludes, the commonest letters
to Browning from parents contained nothing but thanks and
gratitude for the way in which he and his family provided a real
home for the boys, often the only one they had. 'A happy home,
a second home', as so many of them wrote again and again,
themselves often so far away in the hill stations of remotest
India.
    When parents fussed, he was sympathetic; when they were
pleased, he shared their enthusiasms; when they desired he
found them tutors to care for and coach their sons in the
holidays; or better still, if they wished it, he took the boys in the
holidays himself. Every year he went abroad; to Russia, Sweden,
France, Germany, Switzerland, Portugal, Greece, Italy; sometimes with friends, sometimes with pupils, sometimes with his

brother, mother and sisters. He travelled by coach, train, tricycle, by mule, on foot, by steamer and sailing boat. As a tourist he was indefatigable. His *Memories* are full of amusing descriptions of whom he saw and where he visited. His mother reckoned that in one year he travelled 10,000 miles. In particular he loved climbing, often taking pupils with him. On one occasion Archie Lamb (son of a famous romantic figure, Charlie Lamb of the Eglinton Tournament) walked and scrambled with great activity all the way from Chamonix to Stresa in direct defiance of parental wishes. Mrs Lamb had urged Browning before they left, on 4th August 1865, to dissuade Archie from 'dangerous expeditions' – he was not very strong and should not exert himself. Many of the parents fussed terribly. They were always writing to Mrs Browning – whose own health was extremely robust – to warn her about their darlings' requirements. Swimming, football, even cricket were often vetoed because of their violence. William Story's son Waldo was taken away from the Volunteers, much to Browning's secret delight as he hated Warre, the master who ran them, because the parades were so demanding.

Another father, Sir William Gull, wrote that his son was 'weak & timid', for which Browning must make allowances. The sire of Herbert Picton Morris warned that Bertie was 'very peculiar' and required 'gentle and careful handling'. Gambier *père*, writing from Dieppe, observed that his son had a 'stationary condition'. 'I know not why, but so it is.' Sometimes even the Nanny wrote. In a sad series from the Isle of Wight, Nurse Cooper advised Browning ('Dear Hon [rd] Sir' she began) that Mrs Le Marchant was very ill. Her boy, Latimer, must be worrying. Browning must take this into account. They all relied on the Browning family to cosset their sons as if they were at home. Mrs Browning, Browning himself, and his two sisters, Malvina and 'Dick' whose actual name was Mariana, laughed at the parents and did their best; including dispensing when required a detested, nauseous dose of brimstone and treacle.

It was just because of his delight in youth, albeit sometimes not disinterested, that Browning proved to be such a success,

1 '. . . a delicate little boy who sat by the bedroom fire with his book.' OB aged about 4

2 OB as an 'Apostle' at Cambridge, aged 22

3 George Curzon at Eton, aged 16

4 Curzon and Browning in
  Milan, 1878. 'Dear Curzon
  and I were taken together in
  Milan in a group, in an
  affectionate attitude, don't
  you know? (uneasy laugh)
  And just as the man took the
  cap off, Curzon said, "Surely
  that is not your stomach
  pressing against my elbow,
  OB?"' From A. C. Benson's
  Diary, vol 64, p. 59a

both as a teacher as well as a Tutor. As far as he could he made his house, which eventually harboured forty boys, as easy-going and comfortable as possible. While not averse to sporting activities – he encouraged games for the Lower Boys and presented cups for football and cricket – he refused to bow to the cult of athletics which, in mid-Victorian England, was sweeping all traditions before it. The event that assured its popularity was the publication of *Tom Brown's Schooldays* in the summer of 1857. Of course, like every cultural change, it had been approaching for many years, since, indeed the appointment of Arnold as Rugby's headmaster in 1828, to whom the movement is generally ascribed. Yet, the glorification of games, the demanding worship of the team spirit which swept aside individual freedom and broke so many boyish spirits, was totally removed from Arnold's concept – that of the joy of playing together for the sake of God as well as the school, for the glory of the mind as well as the body.

Browning fought this cult vigorously, encouraging his boys to be independent, to play or study just as they chose, to read books of every category, to learn French, German and Italian, and to argue freely on every subject. He banned the traditional sporting prints of Tom Cribb and Jack Mytton, and filled the rooms and passages instead with Arundel engravings of European masterpieces. Casts of statuary, made in Rome – in the early days obtained through Story – stood in suitable corners and alcoves. The then unfashionable works of Brahms and many other modern composers were performed by groups of local musicians. Poetry readings and plays were encouraged. On Sunday nights there were popular debates.

In opposition to the Eton Society, 'Pop', now debased by the worship of athletics into a club for popular swells, chosen for their sporting achievements alone, he instituted a Literary Society to which he invited prominent speakers. Over all presided his mother, a woman of spirit, grace and intelligence who spoke French and German fluently, and who played and taught the harp and piano. Born at the start of the nineteenth century, she brought to the house an old-world charm. All the boys respected and loved her. At meals when they all sat down together, she and Browning and his two sisters who were still only in their early twenties, all behaved with genteel decorum. For a moment, work and games were forgotten; a cheerful, homely, family atmosphere prevailed.

Sex was the only forbidden subject, and even here Browning's approach was quite different to that of his colleagues, dangerously permissive, according to some of them. Arthur Benson, a lifelong friend who, like Browning, returned to Eton to become a famous and popular housemaster, exactly expressed the general attitude, in his book on Eton, *The Myrtle Bough*.[8]

> With regard to moral matters, I have always pursued a simple system; I have tried with new boys, to discover, as simply as possible, whether there has been anything undesirable in the background, have told them, as forcibly as I could, the absolute necessity of good tone of talk and life, without going too much into details. And I have asked boys from time to time, guarding carefully against any attempt to obtain definite information, whether all has gone well. But of course that is *the* heavy cloud over our life, the one dark fear that stalks in the background.

Browning despised this timid approach, and spoke boldly on sexual matters whenever he felt the need to do so. As every boy had his own room he always saw them alone in the evenings; and thus whenever he found it necessary, he was able to try with fatherly concern to make them confess their secret anxieties.

At these times, forgetting himself and his own sins and erotic fantasies, he spoke of a boy's duty to God and the sacred beauty of male virginity with as much conviction as Edward Pusey.[9] His pi-jaws must have been thrilling and memorable, for many boys obliquely refer to them in letters and memoirs written afterwards. His colleagues thought them extremely suspicious, perhaps because they themselves had not the will to follow his example although, secretly, they wished to do so – certainly the case with Arthur Benson. Also, doubtless, they sensed that Browning himself rather enjoyed them.

In loco parentis

The boys' parents, far away, in as much as they worried at all (which they never did about Browning's morals) were only concerned that these sermons, so very difficult for fathers to make, should be given properly at the right time by a man so qualified to do.

Thus, for any number of reasons, Browning's reputation flourished. At about the time of his thirtieth birthday in 1867, many parents and many boys considered his house the best of any in the school. Certainly, his life was happy and full. In these middle years of his mastership, he published the first of his many works, a new edition of Cornelius Nepos. He contributed four major studies to the new *Encyclopaedia Britannica* – on Caesar, Carthage, Dante and Goethe. He wrote for the *Dictionary of National Biography*. He submitted articles and reviewed books in all the leading periodicals. He became known in the scholastic world as an up-and-coming, progressive educator, and enlarged his circle of friends enormously to include many who are still famous – Arthur Sullivan, George Eliot, Walter Pater, Lord Houghton. For perhaps the only time in his career, he was really content and fully aware of it. He considered leaving Eton for Fettes. Now, a great school in Edinburgh, then it was seeking its first headmaster. He asked a friend, Professor Blackie of Edinburgh University: 'Would you advise me to try for the post? Of course Eton is a very delightful place, especially to an Old Etonian, & Eton boys are particularly pleasant to teach & to deal with. I have therefore a full appreciation of the fatness which I should leave in trying for it . . . but I am devoted to the cause of Education & am quite ready to work where I should be most useful.'[10]

An outside view of Eton's 'fatness' was given by Blackie two years later when he went to Eton and stayed with Browning. He wrote to his wife:

FAIREST BEING, Here I am in the elegant and refined seat of taste, learning, conservatism, and wealth, where the masters make £2000 or £4000 or £5000 of clear profit, and where the whole world

41

appears to be walking with silk slippers on silk carpets. My host, Oscar Browning, is a man of large culture, fine taste, and liberal views; his mother is a woman of breadth, decision, and management; and his sister Malvina a genial, frank, laughing and talking, well-constituted English girl . . .[11]

Browning was always self-indulgent, and ever able to find excuses for whatever he did in connexion with anything. He invariably worked extremely hard, and felt no guilt about living comfortably. Not all his friends shared this view, and already one, Warre Cornish (who like Browning, had returned to Eton, and became, eventually, the Vice Provost), had warned him to take his life more seriously; not to allow material delights to blunt his sense of duty and purpose. He had written in 1863:

> Mein Liebster Freund – I do not think you are one of those people who bear prosperity well, and I think that Eton life is so prosperous that it requires double care on your part. You will think that I never change my tune, but it is nevertheless true, however often I may say it, that you are too self indulgent and have much too great a belief in the rectitude of your own intentions & impulses. I have no ascetic ideas about self indulgence, but I am quite sure that you go beyond the right line in the other direction through not caring about consequences . . . That 'laborare est orare' of yours is dangerous, because there are many ways of working, and it does not follow that because you are tired at night that you have done all your duty by day.[12]

This was certainly sound advice, and Browning ought to have taken heed of it. Many others who liked him less repeated it to him and much more bluntly. He ignored them all, to his own detriment. His own conscience was perfectly clear. He dismissed all of them, even Cornish, as blind or prejudiced ignoramuses.

Always the greatest joy of all – far outweighing the 'silken slippers', the mere, mundane, material delights – were the boys themselves, the ones he loved, the ones who really became his friends – the ones he took on trips in the holidays. In a rare series of his own letters (although he must have written thousands, very few seem to have survived) such a friendship with one of his pupils, Gerald Balfour, is nicely described. Gerald Balfour's father was dead which made him susceptible to Browning's influence; his mother was grand, which added to his charm: the daughter of the 2nd Marquess of Salisbury. Although their friendship was perfectly correct, it was also inspired by Gerald's beauty, for Browning considered him very handsome.

'My dear Madam', Browning wrote, in August 1866, 'I have nothing but good to say of your son Gerald . . . He is everything that I could wish in industry, simplicity and affectionateness of disposition . . .' Again, in December, 'Gerald is as satisfactory in all respects as he can possibly be . . . I hope he will not contract a taste for reading *novels* of which I have seen some signs.' Two years later, 'Gerald is I think doing as well as you could possibly wish or desire. He has been first in his division all this half . . . he is a very constant & pleasant companion to me & I can only wish that he will always go on as he is at present . . .' The next year they went to Sicily. 'We had a most delightful tour. I never enjoyed anything more myself and I think that it quite answered his expectations. We were fortunate in everything but weather. I could not possibly have had a pleasanter companion, and I was delighted that I had an opportunity of studying so closely the beauty of his character. He was always cheerful, lively, extremely affectionate and interested in everything we saw . . . His expenses were about £50.' Another letter: 'I hope I do not underestimate the responsibility of conducting his education & I am sure I could not overestimate the pleasure.'

Two years later, 'I am so extremely fond of him that I find it difficult to criticise his character. He really seems to me quite the most remarkable boy I have ever met, both morally & intellectually. He has the most entire purity of mind & character and at the same time is not at all unfitted for contact with the world . . . I quite dread his leaving this half. His friendship has been such a constant help and assistance to me that Eton will appear very different when he has left it.' Lastly, 'I cannot tell you what a pain it is to me to lose his companionship. It will be a long time before I again find a pupil so sensible, so pleasant, so mature & so sympathetic. I only trust that our friendship may not be interrupted and that I may still continue to enjoy a fair amount of his society.'[13]

In fact, the two remained friends for the rest of Browning's long life; but for many weeks after Gerald left, in the summer of 1871, Browning thought of him every day, and felt empty and unconsolable.

CHAPTER IV

The 'violent reformer'

When Browning took over his first house in the autumn of 1864, there were twenty-eight other houses containing a total of eight hundred boys. They were taught by the Head and Lower Master, and eighteen classical assistants who formed the real core of instruction.

Of these, the senior was William Johnson who remains a legendary Eton figure, the illustrious composer of 'Heraclitus' and author of the lyrics of the Eton Boating Song, Browning's elder by fourteen years. He is the most important witness of Browning's life at Eton as a colleague.

Browning, at College, had been his pupil, and had built up, as the letters show, a very special and close relationship. When he returned to the school as a master, aged only twenty-three, really hardly more than a boy, he expected Johnson still to accord him some kind of particular favour.

Johnson did his best for a while, discussing pupils and helping him with his work. He was quite of the same mind with regard to master–pupil relationships: that love is the basis of all morality; that no amount of threatened punishment can encourage a boy as much as affection. So he approved of Browning's informal approach, and did all he could to help and encourage him.

'Rode with Browning,' he wrote in his diary[1] in February 1864.

> Browning more statesmanlike than usual, and very cheerful about his house. He encourages his boys to sit with him after supper till prayers, and talk freely: he tries to teach them history and Whiggery: I am afraid they despise me for my views about the Duke of Wellington. He told me the little he knew about a good cultivated set of boys who hang together, Cook, Gosselin, Barrington, (Everard's friend) etc. etc. We agreed in thinking it very

satisfactory that there should be sets held together by the more feminine sympathies . . .

Such sets were still fashionable, although soon to be swept away by a climate demanding greater manliness. In the 1860s there were yet boys who sent each other perfumed valentines, who spoke to each other by their first names, who, to quote Johnson again, were 'happy and luxurious if not effeminate', who talked to each other 'gushingly like girls'. Boys like these, Johnson liked. Browning had always been too shy to behave like this, at least in public; but as a boy, in his heart of hearts, he may have longed to be able to express such sentiments.

As time went by, their friendship deteriorated. At last, for the only time in his life, Browning received the same treatment that he himself had given so often to favourite boys who had suddenly bored him.

Eton was then in a state of flux. The Parliamentary Commission of Inquiry, the so-called Public Schools Commission which had sat in 1861 and reported in 1864 had recommended a number of changes.

Browning, always a 'violent reformer', to use his own crusading expression, regarded the prospect of change with delight. In his own evidence before the Commission, he had criticised many of Eton's practices, its teaching, curriculum and social traditions, not omitting the Governing Body which, he said, in its ancient form, the form in which it still survived, was obstructive, useless, and quite unnecessary. This, in itself, had given offence. Now the Commission had made its Report, many reforms had become obligatory; many that he himself had advocated. He pressed for them all with missionary zeal, and, with the older members of the staff, not to mention the Provost and Fellows whose powers had all been swept away, he made himself extremely unpopular. After a while even Johnson, who did his best to behave reasonably and was not himself averse to reform, felt obliged to put him in his place.

In the spring of 1869, Browning took up the question of the College Choir. The Commission had said that it ought to be restored, not only because, for three hundred years, the 'sixteen poor choristers' authorised under the Founder's Statutes, had not in fact been appointed at all, but also because, the Commissioners felt, choral music would encourage the boys to behave more seriously in College Chapel. So the choir had been reinstated, but not as Browning considered it should be. Ever ready to go into battle without making a proper reconnaissance he determined, unwisely, to start the attack without first establishing the facts. Johnson warned him not to do it. 'Being persuaded that your interference will cause nothing but irritation in a quarter in which there is already a very strong feeling against young men generally and against yourself in particular, I advise you to do nothing . . .'

Browning, as usual, took no heed, and quite soon, as he might have expected, he received a stern letter from the Provost.

> The Lodge
> Eton Coll
> March 22nd 1869
>
> My dear Browning
>
>   I have been told this morning that you have stated in writing that this College is spending two thousand pounds per annum on the Choir. You will greatly oblige me by informing me a) whether this statement of your words is correct: and, if it be incorrect, b) whether you have named any sum of money as that which the College is now spending upon the Choir, and c) if so, what sum you have named.
>
>   I, as well as other members of the College have no objection to the truth being known on this subject: but we have great objections to exaggerated statements being circulated . . .
>
>   I am, Very truly yours, Charles O. Goodford[2]

Browning, so often to be accused of 'shuffling', seems to have answered rather evasively, and prompted the Provost to write again.

> March 24th 1869
>
> Dear Browning
>
>   In your letter recd yesterday Eve . . . you excused yourself for

stating the large sum of £2000, on the ground that you had no reliable source of information. I ventured to supply some information – but, as your last letter entirely ignored it, I can only conclude that you do not hold it to be reliable. I look in vain for any greater amount of courtesy in this to myself than was shown towards the College . . .

I suppose that you have some reliable information that the College propose spending £2000 per ann upon their Choir. I have not.

I am, Your truly, Charles O. Goodford

Here, for the moment, the matter rested while Browning tilted at other windmills, but later on it arose again.

On this later occasion Dr Goodford who had been at Eton for forty years as pupil, Tutor, Headmaster and Provost, who was loved by all and known as 'The Cogger', whose endless sermons and Dorset burr sent every boy in the Chapel to sleep, at long last lost his temper and gave Browning a stinging rebuke.

At first, he started quietly enough. When Browning raised the question once more, Dr Goodford replied tartly.

November 2nd 1870

Dear Browning

You are quite right in your conjecture. I have not forgotten, nor failed to keep the correspondence to which you refer, but I have really not the time nor the inclination to enter on a refutation of statements which you tell me Dr Hayne made to someone, and someone made to you. When I know your friend's name, I can judge better whether his account is worth my attention. Meanwhile I should like to know the precise time to which you allude, when you say that your friend 'lately' told you.

I am, Yours truly, Charles O. Goodford

Browning, as usual, replied at once, without directly answering the question or making any attempt to apologise. Dr Goodford, really annoyed, retorted with a letter of eight pages.

The 'violent reformer'

November 7th 1870

Dear Browning

I was away from early on Thursday till Sat ^{y} afternoon and unwilling to engage in controversial matters on Sunday.

Your letter of the 3rd has duly reached me – it leaves your informant still anonymous – but incidentally informs me that the word 'lately' in your first note means Tuesday last. For this I thank you. Dr Hayne in a letter of Nov 3 says to me 'I most emphatically deny ever having thought, much less said, that the organ has cost, or is to cost £5000 . . . or that the Choir is the most expensive in England: it is almost a ridiculous thing for me to deny these statements, they are so very far from true'.

The latter part of this sentence I fully endorse. It is really too monstrous to need refutation by figures.

You remind me that our former correspondence was begun by me, not by you. My having kept the correspondence made this reminder unnecessary. I did commence it: I found that you, without a hint to me of what you were doing or taking any steps to ascertain the truth of your statements, had accused me and others of misspending the College funds. I think it not unnatural that I should, under these circumstances, write to you. You tell me that I used strong language of reproach – not unreasonable surely when untrue statements are made of one's conduct to a supposed superior authority though I did not expect, even from you, to find these things repeated in the aggravated form in which they now appear.

Dr Hayne, you say, 'will not tell' you 'what the organ has cost'. Dr Hayne is quite right not to tell you or anybody else what he does not know: if other people who are as, or even more ignorant than he is on this head would be equally discreet they would be more just towards their neighbours, and contribute more to the harmony and happiness of us all.

I am quite ready to give an account and to justify the expenditure of all the College money which has been laid out upon the Choir or the organ to anyone who has a right to ask it of one: but not to gratify the curiosity of those who have no such title to meddle in the matter.

I am, Yours truly, Charles O. Goodford

Browning, as usual, shrugged this off, but, by now, the clouds

were gathering. He argued continually with all his colleagues.
Even Cornish who really loved him and who had warned him so
many years before in the long letter, already quoted, to be less
conceited and self-indulgent, found his attitudes almost
unbearable. He seemed to be hastening into the storm.

He had even broken with William Johnson, writing a long
letter of complaint, firstly about a minor grievance, then as he
did with everyone else, going back on the past history of every
difference they had ever had. Johnson's reply, including a
postscript which he sent really as a second letter, amounted in
all to twenty pages.

A final letter in this series, that is to say in the letters from
colleagues which reveal Browning at his worst, not so much a
'violent reformer' as an almost paranoiac busybody, is one from
Stone, an assistant master.[3] The text is really self-explanatory.
Stone begins 'I opened your letter with some misgiving.' How
many letters that Browning wrote must have provoked a similar
groan as they tumbled through a recipient's mail box – groans
so often echoed by himself at the sight of epistles from certain
parents.

> I opened your letter with some misgiving, but its contents
> reassured me. If I had acted a *prudent* part I suppose I should have
> said nothing about this Committee to you, but I brought it out as
> the most natural thing in the world, knowing that you would take
> an interest in the subject, but never dreaming that your exclusion
> from it would be resented as an injustice. I can assure you, as far as
> my knowledge goes, there was no deliberate purpose in omitting
> your name . . . However this is not, as you will say, the real point at
> issue, whether you are or are not a member of the Committee: what
> you complain of, and feel sore about, is the cause, which you
> imagine has prevented you being selected: namely a deliberate
> personal slight. I can assure you most earnestly that you are
> mistaken, the choice having been made, I believe, hastily & with-
> out exact balancing of claims.
>
> You complain bitterly of want of sympathy. Is this want
> altogether unnatural? A reformer must be prepared to encounter
> it, and the more, as he allows his contempt of existing abuses and

their supporters to escape him. But you will say he ought to expect sympathy from reformers. The worst of it is, that there are many ways of tentative reform, and hence the conservative, who simply sticks to what is, has more chance of sympathy and support than the men, who on this side or that would leave the groove. However strongly you may feel the error of what is, it is essential that you should curb the very natural impatience which the stolid 'vis inertia' of an old fallacy causes, and deal tenderly, & therefore fairly with men who uphold it honestly. You must be prepared to defend your colleagues, even when you cannot conscientiously agree with them, and above all be diffident of your own opinion, however strong your convictions may be.

But if you hold yourself bound to protest against, or undermine and assault openly, existing institutions, I do not say the part you choose is not a noble and a right one (though if I must say 'noble', I would leave out 'undermine',) but I think the man who adopts it must be prepared to do without sympathy to a very great extent, and must find his reward in his work whether it succeed or not. I hope this letter will shew you even by its tediousness, that there is some sympathy to be got, however poor and partial even in be-nighted Eton, and I am sure if you cared to look for it, you would find more.

Yours ever, E.D. Stone.

Stone was correct about the sympathy. When not arguing, Browning was charming – an altogether delightful colleague; for few people had more conflicting sides to their character than he. Many of the things he wished to reform, reforms in fact required by the Commission – a larger staff, smaller classes, revision and modernisation of schoolwork – were agreed by most to be highly desirable. His approach was the thing that upset his colleagues: his overwhelming self-importance, his total blindness to others' feelings, his refusal to listen to con-trary arguments, his pointless persistence in pressing his case which Johnson compared on one occasion to the 'fruitless acti-vity' of a squirrel in a cage. When he was doing something successful like teaching modern European history (which, as it happened, he did supremely) no one ever had stauncher sup-porters. He had taken this on in 1868 when every boy in the

The 'violent reformer'

Upper School had been made to study a modern subject for at least four periods a week. In spite of the extra work it involved, he soon found that in this field, far more than in teaching the classics, he was able to combine his talents as a tutor with his own profound intellectual enthusiasms. Of all the new optional classes, his own at once became the most popular. Quite soon, at many of the other public schools, the success of his work began to be noticed. His views on teaching came to be sought, and his method – the conversational approach, so far removed from the discipline of classics – became the subject of earnest discussion.

In the spring of 1873, Dr Hornby, the school's Headmaster in succession to Dr Balston, decided to curb Browning's historical activities and appoint in his stead a professional historian, not wishing one assistant to become pre-eminent amongst the others. For once Browning's colleagues were aghast, and a great many openly supported him. One of them, Ainger, wrote to Hornby, unofficially speaking for them all.[4]

> A rumour has reached us that you intend to make a change in the history teaching by appointing a special master for the purpose of what has hitherto been done by Browning. Such a master would be either up to the standard of an Oxford history professor, or he would be a young man who had taken a good degree in the school. In the former case we should get more than we want in a place like this without any great increase in the efficiency of the teaching: in the latter it would be most improbable that the teacher would approach the present teacher either in historical attainments, power of imparting knowledge, or influence over the boys forming the class. This seems so obvious to very many of us who have had pupils in Browning's history class, and have been acquainted with the results of it, that we cannot be surprised that he should feel seriously hurt at the prospect of such a supercession. Possibly as compared with a Bryce or a Freeman, Browning's knowledge may be pronounced superficial, but in that or in almost any other literary subject it would be difficult for his habitual critics to substantiate any such charge. For my own part I think he is one of the most cultivated men I ever met, and I cannot comprehend the charge of shallowness so often brought against him. His undertak-

ing the history teaching was an act of voluntary patriotism at a time when it was very much needed. This should entitle it to a somewhat tender consideration even if it had been a failure. Whereas, on the contrary, nothing of late years has been more successful. But behind all this I for one (and I believe many others, but I have no right to speak except for myself) am conscious of a painful feeling at anything which seems to cast a slight on Browning or to lessen his influence. It is, of course, a matter on which opinion may differ, but I do not think you can be aware how many of us feel that more than anything else we owe to Browning's exertions in his own house and pupil-room and in the school generally a very large proportion of any improvement which may have taken place at Eton in the last ten years . . . Our standard in morals, in intellectual pursuits, in everything except athletics, is still miserably low – how low no one can know who is not in daily contact with the frivolity and carelessness about all serious matters which is the prevailing tone. But whatever protest has been made against this muscle worship, whatever effort has been made to promote culture and industry and thereby improve morals, Browning has taken a leading part in it ever since I have known Eton as a master. Again, you came here at a time when changes had to be introduced, and everyone in the place was ready to find fault with them whatever they were. During all this time Browning was your most loyal supporter, much more loyal than many who have always enjoyed a larger share of your confidence. This is so well known to us that we can hardly understand its not being known to you. We younger masters here . . . feel that we cannot do better than follow the example Browning has set us, and which I hope he may long continue to set, for he is by far your most valuable assistant . . . I am well aware that the picture I have drawn may differ from that which some of us would draw, especially as I know from personal experience some of the older men. It is possible, though I have no right to say so, that you hold their views and have been in some degree influenced by them.

Dr Hornby, naturally enough, disliked such protests from junior staff. For some months he stuck to his opinions. What had really put his back up had not been Browning's obvious success but the fact that Browning had started to boast about it. In the end he decided to relent and allowed Browning's classes to continue. Like many activities in Browning's life, especially during his time at Eton, many years were destined to pass before his work was superseded and his place taken by any successor with an equal gift for teaching.

5 Eton in the late 19th century. Browning's is the first tall house in the middle distance on the right .

6 Browning kicked out by Doctor Hornby. A contemporary cartoon with superimposed photographs

7 OB in his prime at Cambridge in the 1890s

CHAPTER V

Greek love and George Curzon

Another aspect of Browning's life in these years of his Tutorship at Eton is revealed in a further series of letters, quite different from any of the others from the Provost, colleagues, parents or boys. They are all from a single correspondent, starting in 1868 and ending in 1872. Their author was the painter Simeon Solomon who shared with Browning a common interest in what was known as 'Greek Love'. Because such love was widely practised by many people in the nineteenth century, especially members of the Oxford Movement; because it was thought to be innocent and good; and because it often led to disaster, a pause must be made to consider its history and ethic.

Its literary origin was found in Greece as expressed in two of Plato's Dialogues, that of Phaedrus, the friend of Socrates, and the one which follows it, known as the *Symposium*. In these the qualities of love are discussed. The participants agree that its highest form is found in the love of men for each other. This view became a cult with its own extensive and arcane literature, part of a wider change in fashion generally known as the Aesthetic Movement. The Movement's philosophy, that life is short and must be lived to the fullest intensity, that only the senses really matter, that Art must exist for Art's sake and not for any other purpose, suited people like Browning perfectly. In all this there was nothing new, but the widespread expansion of public schools which provided a classical education to a huge, new section of society – the expanding, prosperous middle class – furnished, also, a new field in which Platonic love could flourish.

The muscular athletes who became heroes to the Lower boys provided a perfect contemporary parallel with the military élite of Sparta and Athens to whom youths were attached as cadets; while the popular passion for mediaeval life in which every prefect longed to be a knight, and every fag hoped to be his page, gave to a suspect Greek relationship the convenient blessing of Christianity.

For those who wished to live to the full there were real arguments for 'Greek Love'. Just because it was self-sufficient and not a step towards procreation, it had to remain a romantic relationship. It gave rise to intense emotions, out of which, as everyone knew, magical works of imagination in prose, poetry, music and painting were often mysteriously created.

In the public schools and universities these passions were seething just as Browning left Cambridge and returned as a junior master to Eton. Any homosexual tendencies which he may have enjoyed in secret previously were suddenly given a code of practice which exactly suited his personal demands. Boy-love was harmless and beautiful. Added to which it could lead to attachments which might bind the lovers together in a lifelong friendship.

With such affairs, of course, there were dangers. In pederastic paintings and literature, Lust was always the enemy of Love, and as often as not it emerged victorious. One of Solomon's best-known paintings was of 'Love dying by the breath of Lust'. His only book, a prose poem of his Spirit's journey towards perfection, led by his disembodied Soul in the guise of a naked, effeminate youth, describes meeting the spirit of Passion. Passion had sought to slay Love, and became in the end the 'Paramour of Hate'.

Browning was perfectly familiar with this, but cheerfully dismissed it as fanciful irrelevance. When in 1873 Solomon was caught in a public lavatory committing an offence with a man named Roberts, Browning at least was really horrified. Most of Solomon's fellow aesthetes – Pater, Swinburne, Rossetti, Morris – became alarmed and cruelly dropped him. Browning, also, cast him aside, and their correspondence stopped abruptly. Browning used, later, to boast of his friendship; but that was after fifty years when Solomon's name was returning to the fore as a gifted, forgotten Pre-Raphaelite painter whose early works were becoming fashionable. Browning was then an octogenarian, and Solomon was safely dead.

Greek love and George Curzon

Simeon Solomon's letters to Browning begin in the autumn of 1868, shortly after they had first met, brought together by the poet Swinburne whom Solomon had known for some years. They met at the home of Richard Moncton Milnes, Lord Houghton, politician and man of letters, who was well known in homosexual circles for his fine collection of erotic books. Solomon's letters clearly show a strong, immediate, mutual attraction.

It was not long before he was at Eton, gushing over the beauty of the boys, and not long before he and Browning addressed each other by their christian names, a familiarity at that time only adopted by members of a family and a few extremely intimate friends. In the whole of Browning's personal archive of approximately 10,000 correspondents there is only a handful of similar cases.

In the spring they went to Italy together although Browning, travelling with Balfour, continued onwards to Sicily. Simeon Solomon stayed in Rome, falling in love with an unknown Roman youth, who probably became the dedicatee of his 'Vision of Love revealed in Sleep' conceived in Rome in that year.

All the boys that Browning admired were now available for Solomon's delight, both those who were still at Eton and also those who had gone to Oxford. At Oxford Browning knew Walter Pater, the High Priest of the Aesthetic Movement, with whom he also shared the names of his beloveds, and whom Solomon often visited.

'How is the dear slim angel out of the circular Botticelli?' Solomon wrote to Browning after a visit to Oxford, referring to George Lawrence, a boy at Eton, to whom Browning was much attached. 'Present my spiritual kiss to him if you please, and also to Julian Story and the sad beauty of the Bank. Do you keep a thermometer for testing love at Eton? I think you should, for I am certain that Love proceeds from one person to another in waves on the air – at Oxford I should think it would always be 110 in the shade and thousands in the sun.'[1]

In another letter he wrote,

The news about the 15th-century angel is most distressing, also the other things you tell me. I wish you could convert, purify and purge in the fires of Love that issue from your dear eyes the person at the Bank, I am sure such a mouth would be worth the trouble. Balfour should be beaten, he should be scourged with rods of iron. Pray, my dear Oscar, beat him till the wings, which are latent in his shoulder blades, sprout. I have chosen two of the photos you were so sweet as to send me, although they are not altogether satisfactory. I want to draw you when you come to London, as the Bridegroom in the Song of Songs. I shall crown you with a circlet of embracing loves, and the Spikes shall be represented by wings and myrtles. Being caused to fly swiftly, I touch you at the time of the evening oblation.

I hope your Mother and sisters are quite well, please remember me very kindly to them. Goodbye.

Yours affect, S. Solomon.

Other letters in the same vein are sprinkled throughout the correspondence. Solomon sketched Browning twice, and also made him a personal bookplate, now a scarce collector's item. Browning always liked the drawings and published one of them in his *Memories*.

No doubt Simeon knew all about 'Greek Love' [Browning wrote in a private letter many years later]. [He] talked about it and joked about it but it is not within my knowledge that he ever practised it. I took him to Rome to paint a picture of Melchizedek, which he was too lazy ever to begin. He fell in love with a boy, who was, I believe, good and innocent and made a beautiful drawing of him of which he gave me a copy – but so far as I know nothing more. The story about Xacis is probably true, but his degradation was due to drink and that was entirely caused by his intimacy with that little beast Swinburne. They were never *friends*, they talked nothing but smut. Their connection came to an end because no friendship can be founded on lust and drunkenness. Their vices were *Sadic* not Greek. His only real friends apart from artists were Pater and myself whom he really loved and we loved him. Simeon was certainly not good looking, rather the reverse, he was thick and not physically impressive. He was very Jewish but not of an attractive type.

58

Greek love and George Curzon

Few people know that the aesthetic movement which had so much influence in England from Ruskin to Oscar Wilde had as one of its characteristics a passionate desire to restore 'Greek Love' to the position which its votaries thought it ought to occupy. They believed that bisexual love was a sensual and debasing thing and the love of male for male was in every way higher and more elevating to the character. I was interested, but did not agree with them and, as I was at that time a schoolmaster, it was absolutely impossible that I should take their view of things.[2]

Whatever Browning may have said, it is clear that he and Solomon were intimate and enjoyed a more than normal friendship. Solomon's letters abundantly prove it.

With boy-love the latent problem is always the passage of time, especially so in the lives of schoolmasters whose loves not only cease to be young, start to sprout beards and to lose their voices, but also actually go away. In Browning's case, especially with Balfour, this metamorphosis was really painful. Solomon sympathised, and tried to comfort him. 'I wish Balfour wouldn't get so long, his head gets smaller and smaller – come to town – let us go to a concert and have a very very select evening.' When Balfour left, Browning was distressed. 'Poor widowered Oscar,' wrote Solomon.

Solomon's letters conclude the collection of those from friends outside the school, written during the fifteen years of Browning's assistant mastership at Eton. It is evident from his nephew Wortham's biography that there must have been many many more, some from Pater in particular. All these seem to be lost. The picture of his life is clear, however, especially his concern with 'Greek Love' and the lengths to which he thought he should pursue it. An interesting paper which escaped destruction is a pamphlet, possibly written by himself (since no specialist in this field can ascribe another author to it), which praises the nobility of boy-love and extolls the kiss exchanged by lovers as a pure act, entirely permissible.

And here, incidentally, I will say something on a practice which has always been thrown in our teeth as conclusively providing a sensual passion – I mean kissing. It has been denounced as impure by vigorous opponents, while even the mildest remonstrance stigmatizes it as sinful: yet we fail to see where the impurity can be associated with it, except in the minds of its denouncers, or where the sin exists except in the practice of the hypocrite who so piously warns us against vicious habits. A kiss is the pledge of love, and must therefore be admissible wherever lawful love exists: how then can men argue that a kiss makes that love unlawful? Effeminacy, too, has been charged on us boy-lovers who delight to win kisses from our loves: to which I can only answer that our accusers must have extended the meaning of that word considerably, to make such an application possible. As for us, we are not ashamed to kiss each other: we glory in that long embrace in which the souls of two lovers meet and unite on their lips, and seal the faith which those lips have vowed.

[He concludes with an unexpected burst of jingoism.] We claim the right of English gentlemen, to be treated as gentlemen, not to be suspected and accused of vices which we ourselves have the most reason to abhor. We demand that our innocence should be admitted till our guilt is proved. And to all true boy-lovers we say 'Come forward boldly, and stand up to defend your love. Show these men the falseness and foulness of their slanders: show them what love can be, what love can do. Is this a time to shrink back and hesitate? God is on our side, the God who himself has bestowed on us this most precious gift; and if God be for us, who can be against us?'[3]

Whoever may have written this pamphlet, it expressed Browning's view exactly, at least during his time at Eton. To love boys in a spiritual manner was entirely good and perfectly innocent. To exchange kisses was equally harmless. It was nothing more than a natural desire to prove a mutual affection.

In April 1872, his former tutor and colleague, Johnson, was dismissed for writing a letter to a boy which was intercepted by the boy's father and brought to the attention of Dr Hornby. It was said that Johnson had decided to retire but everyone knew the truth was otherwise. Solomon heard the news from Browning, visiting Eton shortly afterwards, and passed it on to his friend, Swinburne. The whole school was agog with the drama:

'Have you heard that Johnson has left and changed his name to Cory?' he wrote. 'It is creating a sensation . . .'

Then, only ten months later, in February 1873, came Simeon Solomon's own disaster, his arrest and actual committal to prison for a public act of gross indecency which was soon known to everyone at Eton.

At this point Browning should have paused and taken stock of his reputation. Already his friendship with Walter Pater had given rise to gossip and suspicion. Now his association with Solomon put him in a really dangerous position. Yet he continued to behave as usual, making himself increasingly unpopular with the Governing Body and many of the staff – most of all with Dr Hornby who was more and more disturbed by his activities. He was always trying to change the curriculum, always late in taking his classes, always proposing impossible reforms, always infringing the regulations. He was troublesome, too, in other ways. He held private concerts and theatricals which Hornby considered a waste of time, and invited controversial figures to speak at the school Literary Society which he himself had founded earlier. John Ruskin came twice and presumed to criticise Alfred Tennyson, then at the height of his popularity, daring to call *The Princess* 'useless', and the hero of *Maud* 'an ass and a fool'.

Worst of all, and most embarrassing, Browning led his own crusade against the prevailing homosexuality, encouraged, he said, by the playing of games and the barbarous cult of admiring the body, letting it be known throughout the school that any boy in any difficulty might safely come to him for guidance; at the same time, accosting personally, any charming or handsome boy who was said by others to be courting danger, drawing him aside and giving him advice.

In vain his friends told him to be careful, warned him that Hornby was losing patience, urged him to curb his zeal for reform, especially towards the boys' morals which, they said, was causing comment.

He refused to listen to a word from anybody. His critics, he replied, were prudes and busybodies. They were just jealous of his personal success. Ever since he had been a housemaster his artistic interests and moral principles had always been misinterpreted.

In the spring of 1873, the very spring of Solomon's arrest, he found he was teaching a boy called Curzon, a boy he had met the previous summer taking an extra class for a colleague, and in whom he took an immediate and delighted interest.

Curzon was handsome as well as clever – best of all, he was the son of a peer, the 4th Baron Scarsdale of Scarsdale, head of one of the oldest families in England. Since Curzon's house was known to be rather lax morally, and since his Tutor, Wolley-Dod, was not renowned for intellectual prowess, he seemed to Browning to need protection as well as scholastic encouragement.

Browning's argument for such a course – that of taking him under his wing even though he was not in his house – had its own unanswerable logic. Boys who showed athletic promise were taken up by athletic masters and coached for hours in the nets or boats, no matter who their Tutors might be; therefore, lads who were promising scholars should be taken up and coached by himself in as many subjects as might be expedient for as many hours as they liked in his library, no matter who were their actual Tutors. As to the problem of moral danger, this, of course, was another matter. In his view, in a case like this where a clever boy was also attractive, he would always do his best to warn and advise him.

Browning's love-affair with Curzon – for such, in fact, it really was, however much he tried to deny it – became suddenly a *cause célèbre* in the summer of 1874 when Curzon was accidentally hit in the eye by a cricket ball. For some months Curzon's Tutor had been annoyed by Browning's behaviour, his invitations to Curzon to meals, his interference with the boy's work, his habit of sending personal messages. He was finally pushed beyond disapproval when (due to the cricket ball accident which kept Curzon away from sport and gave him leisure in the afternoons) Browning showed off the wounded Curzon in public by taking him out for an afternoon drive in his carriage.

Greek love and George Curzon

As often happened in Browning's life, a quite small, tactless act annoyed his colleagues so extremely that they hit back with unexpected vigour. Wolley-Dod was so enraged by Browning's effrontery that he went immediately to Dr Hornby. He, after all, was Curzon's Tutor, and he was the one who should take him for drives if sickness prevented him playing cricket.

Dr Hornby sent for Browning, and after making the cryptic remark that he heard Curzon was a handsome boy, which he then immediately tried to retract, he ordered Browning to stop seeing him. He concluded the interview with a stern lecture on the general dangers of assistant masters making too much of comely youths, even in the cause of protecting their morals. It was all-important to prevent gossip, especially when dealing with delicate questions.

Browning was wounded and also furious. The captain of Curzon's own house had warned him that the boy was in moral danger and had sought his advice as to what to do about it; and Curzon's own father and mother whom he happened to know through another parent had told their son to go and see him. He had never done anything but good for Curzon. He had saved him from all the moral dangers that boys with good looks are likely to encounter, for which on many, many occasions Curzon himself had actually thanked him. He had so successfully encouraged his work, and so enlarged his general knowledge, that in all subjects his improvement was applauded. As to the accusation of 'spooning' of which he learnt he was being charged, he denied it immediately and categorically. Spooning was the slang word in use at the time for what, in fact, he was doing; sentimentally falling in love. His friendship, he said, was entirely platonic; a rare example of a perfect union between a master and a pupil.

At first, therefore, he declined to promise that all contact should cease between them. Going over Hornby's head, he appealed to the Provost to back him up, and when the latter refused to do so, he persuaded Curzon's father to write, and later on to visit Hornby in another attempt to make him relent.

In every case, his efforts failed. It was not for nothing that Dr

Greek love and George Curzon

Hornby was sometimes compared to King Log, the lifeless monarch in Aesop's fables. Over Curzon he remained inflexible. He demanded a promise in writing from Browning that the latter should entirely cease to see him. In the end, Browning gave in; for Hornby offered him a simple choice. Do as he was told or accept dismissal.

It was now obvious to all the staff, and to everyone else who cared to think about it, that Browning's time as an Eton housemaster was very rapidly coming to an end. It was quite certain that Hornby suspected him – in fact he said so to some of his colleagues – of being, if not a homosexual at least an extremely dangerous influence. Only Browning himself continued in a state of uneasy hope and blindness; unwisely trusting that things would get better; naively supposing that no one suspected his secret longings for boys like Curzon just because he managed to suppress them. He seriously thought of resignation, and discussed it at length with George Eliot, an old friend whose opinion he valued. Like nearly everybody outside Eton, she knew nothing at all of his actual behaviour, and strongly urged him to stay where he was. He wished to do so and was easily persuaded. He returned to Eton after the holidays and, in spite of the public humiliation of often seeing Curzon in the street and not being able even to greet him, he determined to pretend that nothing had happened.

Curzon's father had written to him warmly.[4]

Kedleston
Derby
July 14th 1874

Dear Mr Browning

I exceedingly regret this very unpleasant complaint of Mr Wolley Dod's, with reference to your conduct towards my son George. I am fully aware of your warm feelings & keen desire that he should grow up a manly, true, pure-minded lad, & though it is possible that your notice of him may have tended to annoy his Tutor, I give you full credit for acting from the purest motives, & I do not wish the kindly relations between you & my boy to fall through. I quite believe that you were instrumental in rescuing

George from companions of more than doubtful repute, & that your sole desire & object has been to elevate & improve his character. I have had a kind letter from Mr Hugessen on this matter (for he too takes a warm interest in George) & I can only hope that no further unpleasantness may ever occur on this head – thanking you for so full an explanation of the circumstances, believe me, yrs very truly, Scarsdale

It was not in Browning's nature, however, to walk in the path of duty if he wished to stray beyond its borders. He soon gave Dr Hornby another example of impossible behaviour, and a further occasion to reprimand him.

For years it had been a regulation that no master, with a house or otherwise, should tutor more than forty pupils. An unexpected official check in the year following the Curzon incident revealed that Browning had forty-three. As soon as this was pointed out, he applied for a temporary dispensation which the Provost granted on the understanding that when it expired at the end of the summer it would not be renewed as a matter of course. It would have to be asked for and granted again.

Browning, typically forgot to ask for it, and when he returned at the end of the holidays and finally applied for a further renewal, the Governing Body refused to approve it.

With characteristic, naive egoism, he called immediately on Dr Hornby to ask him to plead his case with the Provost. He had, as usual, excellent arguments. He would lose money by the prohibition, for a lost pupil was a lost fee; he would cause the pupils harm and distress, since changing tutors was always upsetting; he would give the impression of being victimised since other colleagues, as Hornby knew, had already been given the necessary authority.

There are sometimes moments in the life of a chief who has to deal with contentious subordinates when patience snaps and reason departs. So it was with Dr Hornby when Browning came that morning to see him. Normally bland, charming, urbane, the Headmaster suddenly lost his temper. He flew at Browning with ungovernable rage, and told him exactly what he thought of him. He called him a liar and a shuffling troublemaker. He listed every broken rule, every infringement of the regulations, every seditious act and remark which Browning had made since 1868 when he, Hornby, had taken over, a period of more than seven years. The matter of the pupils was the last straw. He categorically refused to condone it. Browning had shuffled for the last time, and must accept the inevitable consequences.

To behave like this was understandable, but to give Browning peremptory notice, which is what he did the following day, had the appearance of being unreasonable. If he had made up his mind to sack him he ought to have given a better excuse, for Browning's error in being late in his application for extra pupils was really only a technicality. No one even then believed it. However, on these grounds he dismissed him. The last day of the current half was to mark the end of Browning's Eton appointment.

Everyone outside Eton was stunned, and even Browning himself was incredulous. A major row was now inevitable. Hornby was faced with a difficult decision: to tell the truth and let Browning be damned, or stick to his lie and be damned himself.

If he lost, as he possibly might; if the Provost and Fellows failed to support him and ordered Browning's reinstatment, he would then, obviously, have no choice but to pack his bags and depart instead of his assistant.

CHAPTER VI

'Ruined and disgraced'

The Reverend James John Hornby, DD, DCL, to give him his full title and distinctions, was born in 1826, the second son of a Westmorland family which was well connected and also distinguished. His father, Sir Phipps, was an admiral, his mother the daughter of a famous general. By a curious genealogical twist he was thrice related to the Earls of Derby. He enjoyed thus, according to his times, an impeccable social standing.

He had qualifications which were every bit as good as his position. He had taken a first in classics at Oxford, and also won a blue as an oar, having previously, when at Eton, been a member of the eleven at cricket. He was, too, a mountaineer, with several notable first ascents to his credit.

In appearance, he was well built, not particularly tall or handsome, but with a presence which was both inspiring as well as amiable. Wherever he went he was well liked, and in great demand as an after-dinner speaker, an art in which he especially excelled. His only fault was a certain weakness which made him loath to take decisions. When he had made one, he would not change it. He was also weak as a disciplinarian, though strong in the hand when it came to punishment. The arms which had swung the bat at Lord's, had dipped the oar so well in the Thames, and gripped the alpenstock so firmly, were kept in continual trim by the use of the birch.

The first Headmaster to come from Oxford, the first ever to be appointed without a previous tour as an assistant, the first to be both a scholar and an athlete, he had been received with acclamation. The Captain of the School had given him a birch, elegantly tied with pale blue ribbons according to the immemorial custom, and all the staff had gathered to greet him; all, that is, except Oscar Browning. Browning had merely sent him a telegram. He had been delayed abroad with a pupil with whom he had gone on tour in the holidays. Apparently stranded without their luggage, they had been compelled to linger in the south of France.

If Hornby's social and scholastic standing was better than Browning's; if, too, being ten years older and a clergyman, Hornby's words carried more weight, when it came to the battle of dismissal in the winter of 1875 he found Browning, none the less, an active and capable adversary. Browning had some excellent cards. For a start he was widely known to the public, almost better known than Hornby, because of his personal contact with parents. Many of these were as influential as any supporters of Dr Hornby; many, also, were acquainted with Browning far better than they were with Hornby simply because they had boys in his house. Then there was Browning's reputation as a pioneer of education, as one of the generation of teachers who desired many radical reforms, more flexible methods and curricula, less emphasis on rigid timetables, more importance given to the arts, less time devoted to athletics. In this field he was well respected and, as events were soon to prove, he had the ear of assistant masters in public schools throughout the country. He was, in other words, an opponent who was more than able to fight effectively, not a mere trembling subordinate who would slink away and admit he was wrong the moment his faults were authoritatively pointed out to him.

His obvious difficulty was as someone attacking an entrenched establishment, a manoeuvre that is often unpopular and always dangerous. That a man with his temperament, a widely suspected homosexual, could not wisely be allowed to remain in any boarding school at all – the real reason behind his dismissal and weakness in his defence – never entered his imagination.

Always convinced of his own rectitude, never able to accept criticism, totally unaware of the dubious impression he gave to all experienced men of the world when they saw him cuddling handsome pupils, he thought merely that Hornby was prejudiced. Forced suddenly to fight for his life, he set about it with vigorous indignation, defending his past record in the school with an air of astonished and persecuted innocence.

For the first weeks after his dismissal, until the early days of

'Ruined and disgraced'

October, Browning kept the matter to himself. He told only his mother and sisters, and an old friend, Knatchbull-Hugessen, a Liberal Member of Parliament for Kent, whose son would have come to Browning's house if matters had gone according to plan. He wrote a long letter to Hornby, rebutting all the different charges that the latter had made at the time of the interview, and spent his everyday life in a trance, hardly able to converse or teach. When he learnt that Hornby was adamant, that go he must without appeal, he felt, for a moment, quite confused, like one who awakes from a deep sleep in unfamiliar surroundings.

His first act, on regaining his spirit, was to write a circular letter to his colleagues, telling them about his dismissal, and warning them about the danger in which they, too, must be standing: of similar dismissal without appeal. Then he wrote to all the parents of the boys already boarding in his house, and to all those to whom he was committed – he had promised places years in advance – giving an explanation of what had happened.

Only a man of Browning's conceit could have taken the response as calmly as he did. All but two of the assistant masters signed a memorial to Dr Hornby expressing their consternation and regret; and thirty-five of the boys' parents also signed a letter of protest, addressed not only to Dr Hornby but also to the Governing Body. At the same time, they wrote to Browning, as did many of his colleagues and pupils. Some of their letters are really interesting. All show a sense of dismay, and not one overtly reveals the actual reason behind the disaster. Yet, reading between the lines, with today's knowledge of human psychology, it is easy to see the secret fear that lurked in the back of their minds as well as in Hornby's.

The Headmaster of Harrow, Dr Butler, an old friend from Cambridge, in a long letter[1] wrote,

We have often talked over the moral dangers of Public Schools, and the close connection in all large masses of boys between intellectual ardour and moral purity. That you were unmistakably in earnest on the right side was a conviction very dear to my heart; a conviction which added much in my eyes to the value of your friendship. That your connection with Eton should have to be severed, and severed in this distressing manner, is a thought on which I do not like to dwell.

A former young colleague at Eton, S.H. Butcher, wrote,

You have indeed fought the battle of culture against an engrossing athleticism or would-be gentlemanly nonchalance but you have done much more. Culture and moral indifference sometimes go together. But I cannot too strongly express how much I believe morality is indebted to you and to your courageous struggles against all that was vile, though not always condemned by public opinion.

Browning's old friend Cornish, still an Eton colleague, told him,

I wish particularly to bear witness to the example which your house has afforded to the School. You have been able by your own efforts and the help of your family, to keep up a domestic relation between yourself and your boys, which is rare even in the best houses; and this has contributed greatly to the excellent order and harmony, as well as the high tone, moral and mental, which marks your house. It has for many years stood deservedly among the very first houses at Eton; and it will be a real calamity to the School if its unity should be broken up and its tradition lost.

Browning's beloved pupil Balfour, by then a graduate of Trinity, Cambridge, assured him the moment he heard the report,

I was shocked and distressed beyond measure at hearing the news of your dismissal. Surely the Head-Master cannot have realized the gravity of his resolve. I know he has persistently misconceived your motives and misread your character. But setting aside the individual hardships of the case, what an injury would be inflicted on the School by your departure! Of your efforts against immorality I need say nothing: they are notorious to all who are acquainted with the real condition of Eton and capable of an intelligent interest in its improvement.

'Ruined and disgraced'

Another Etonian, Frank Money, who retained a lifelong friendship with Browning, put the matter more explicitly.

> ... you have a certain rare and delicate gift, which you use to the noblest ends, of drawing towards you many who are seldom drawn towards anyone. It must be evident to anyone who has any perception of the different dispositions that exist in the intense natures of boys, that such a gift may be the means of causing in a School a very large leaven of purity and virtue. It is a matter of ordinary experience to those who know anything of psychology that those who have the greatest capabilities of good are also the most prone to evil; that where there is any 'fervid artistic temperament, there is often a fervidly passionate physique.' To such boys Eton has peculiar dangers: to such boys routine, regulations, admonitions, are often perfectly useless: but who ever knew such natures unyielding to the gentle guidance of a heart that sympathizes, a mind that ennobles, and a friendship that purifies? In this way you have, Mr. Browning, led many ...

Lastly a father, Lord Portsmouth, expressed the sentiment of most of the parents,

> I can strongly attest that the love of work, the anxiety to improve themselves and the right feeling which is apparent, I am happy to say, in my three sons, is very much the result of your good influence. I think that your leaving Eton would be a great loss to the School. In fact, I look upon it that your removal would prove an irreparable loss to Eton. The tone of your house is so manly and straightforward.

During all this time the Governing Body had not convened to consider the problem although many had received letters from Browning himself, from boys and parents, and, of course, from Dr Hornby. Hornby even more than Browning must have awaited their meeting with keen impatience.

They met at last on November 9th. Although no minutes exist of the conversations that passed between them, Hornby was asked to present a statement which he did at length the following day and which included an account of the Curzon

71

love-affair. Curzon's actual name was omitted, but Hornby is bound to have given it orally. As a result, the Board decided – considering also the other complaints of slackness in work and insubordination – that Hornby had acted within his rights, and declined to interfere.

On hearing this, Knatchbull-Hugessen whom Browning had kept informed from the very beginning, and who had already warned Hornby that sooner or later he might publish the facts and air the matter in the House of Commons if Hornby was not prepared to compromise, decided the time had come to write to the newspapers. Dr Hornby had refused to reveal what he had said to the Governing Body and malicious rumours were getting about that Browning was actually being sacked for a worse offence than disobedience. Hugessen had perfect trust in Browning, and had no idea of the truth of the rumours. He hoped an appeal to public opinion would force Hornby to produce his statement. Convinced that Hornby was dismissing Browning out of pure spite and petty-mindedness, he determined to use his considerable influence as an MP and public figure to make the Reverend Doctor change his mind.

So a long letter from Knatchbull-Hugessen appeared in all the principal daily newspapers. The *Morning Post* gave it six columns, and the other papers nearly as much, all of them also at the same time, considering the matter in lengthy editorials.

As often happens in human struggles, the result was not entirely as planned. To Browning's and Hugessen's mortification, only the Liberal *Daily News* called the matter a 'serious dispute' and said that Browning was 'of some distinction'. The others, especially the Tory *Standard*, spoke merely of 'an Eton squabble', and referred to Browning as 'somewhat affected' – a clear reference for those who knew him and disapproved of the cult of aestheticism, to his obvious homosexual tendencies. *The Times* was extremely critical, deploring with 'Quondam Etonensis', an anonymous contributor who joined the fray, that 'these quarrels' and 'displays of temper' did nothing but harm to the College and the boys, and describing Browning as 'notoriously troublesome'. Dr Hornby kept his peace. The only letter

'Ruined and disgraced'

to be published from Eton was about the recent extensive floods – assuring parents that in spite of these, none of the boys was in any danger from unassimilated sewage.

It was clear that the game was nearly up; the half was ending in a month's time, and Browning would have to leave, find a home for his mother and sisters, and worst of all, be nearly penniless. He decided to make a last effort, if not to get himself reinstated, at least to get the Governing Body to grant him a reasonable pension. He had just completed fifteen years, the minimum requirement under the statutes.

The Provost and Fellows scarcely considered it. They were not in the mood to grant any favours, especially after the hubbub in the newspapers; and as their chairman was Dr Goodford who, of course, knew Browning well and had not forgotten the latter's criticisms over the cost of the choir and the organ, they rapidly decided to inform him that no pension whatever could be granted.

On almost the last day of the year, Monday 27th December, just before he finally left, Browning decided to write to the Provost, not this time in any hope that Dr Hornby or anyone else could be made now to change their minds, but simply to put the facts on record as he himself so resentfully saw them. He reviewed his case for twenty pages, finishing up in bitterness and sorrow.[2]

My house, although perhaps neither you or the H.M. were aware of it, was one of the best if not the best in the college. I had spent upon it ten years of assiduous labour. It was never better than at the present moment, in discipline, intelligence, mutual affection & devotion to myself. It contained in it a large proportion of boys destined to do honour to the school; many more of distinguished ability were on my list. The two captains of my house were the best scholars among the oppidans, the only oppidans likely to be selected for the Newcastle. All this fabric, an integral part of the organism of the school, is violently destroyed beyond the possibility of reconstruction. I could never see my boys together at any time last half without feeling to the full the wicked folly that doomed such a family to dispersion.

The year ended. Browning left. His mother and sisters closed the house. His long, long, letter to the Provost remained like his own career at Eton, unappreciated and unrequited. Dr Goodford never replied.

If that was the end of the matter for Browning, it was not so for Knatchbull-Hugessen. He was not accustomed to being abused in the national newspapers – he had been described as 'utterly incompetent', and otherwise insulted by 'Quondam Etonensis' – also in Browning's dismissal he very rightly observed a flaw in the Public Schools Act of 1868 which ought, he believed, to be amended. Under the thirteenth clause of the Act an assistant in any public school had no right of appeal from dismissal.

On April 7th the following year he laid a Petition before the House of Commons from one hundred and six assistants from the seven great public schools to which the Act in question referred. These were Winchester, Eton, Westminster, Shrewsbury, Harrow, Rugby, Charterhouse. It stated 'That your Petitioners are, by the 13th clause of the Public Schools Act of 1868, liable to be summarily dismissed from office at the pleasure of their respective head masters.' It went on to aver that they felt an increasing sense of insecurity in this situation, and prayed the House to afford them such relief as it might in its wisdom see fit. Hugessen proposed a Select Committee to consider whether any change should be made.

Edward Hugessen Knatchbull-Hugessen was one of those industrious men on whom the House of Commons depends to carry the daily burden of work who are not, in spite of being clever, gifted with any outstanding ability. Born in 1829, the sixth son of a Kentish baronet, he had been to Eton and then to Oxford where for a term he was President of the Union Debating Society. Then, in 1857, he had been elected to the House of Commons as a Liberal member for a local constituency. He was generally liked in the House of Commons in spite of an aspect of dismal gravity, and was well known in Society salons as the author of popular books for children. Only the nannies had ever read them, but that was really of no importance. His latest effusion had just come out, with the daunting title of *Higgledy-Piggledy*. Jane Austen had been his aunt. It must be said, however, that he lacked her ability.

His Petition ended in complete disaster. To begin with, the House was thinly attended, and bored to death before he began. To make things worse, he presented his argument at such length and so diffusely that, as one of his opponents said, if he had had a case at all, by the time he sat down he had quite destroyed it. This speaker was Sir Robert Anstruther, the head of an ancient Scottish family with a long record of public service who had four intelligent and manly sons. The eldest, Ralph, had been at Eton, in fact had actually boarded at Browning's. He had, of course, when questioned by his father, told him all about Browning and Curzon. Sir Robert, therefore, had a secret weapon. He demolished the innocent Hugessen easily. He had never had any time for aesthetes, and had always been suspicious of Browning. He firmly supported Dr Hornby and the general right of all headmasters to dismiss their staff without interference. The motion, he said, was a great mistake. It should never have been put down.

Browning suffered another defeat just before he parted from Eton, before, in fact, Knatchbull-Hugessen presented his motion in the House of Commons. Just as the year had drawn to a close, in December 1875, University College School, an important, modern, London day-school with almost seven hundred pupils, had announced it required a new headmaster.

With his usual blindness and self-righteous optimism, Browning decided at once to apply for it. Of course, from the start, his chance was nil. No sensible board of governors would ever have appointed any applicant who had just left Eton under a cloud, whatever the brilliance of his testimonials. The letters he presented were certainly outstanding. They made him appear to be a paragon of unbelievably perfect character. Dons, headmasters, peers and lawyers – some of them actually Fellows of Eton – wrote of his qualities with such enthusiasm that it seemed as though they were trying to obtain the post for Browning to salve their own uneasy consciences. When he learnt that he had not succeeded, with characteristic self-satisfaction he had their letters bound in a book. By then it was March and he had left Eton. He had taken his mother and sisters to Leipzig. Never at home without male companions, he had taken also four pupils with whom he worked and walked and talked. They were all boys who had been in his house and who were on the point of leaving for Oxford or Cambridge in the autumn. For the last time as a boys' tutor, this supreme joy was granted him.

The letters home from one of the boys, George Barnes who lived in Surrey, still remain in the family archives and give an interesting and clear account of exactly how they spent their lives. They rose at seven and took exercise. Whenever they could, they went swimming, a sport which Browning always enjoyed, as he liked to undress before an audience, loved to peep at the bodies of others, and delighted in jokes about modesty and shame. He often told the tale of Luigi, the saintly founder of Frankfurt Cathedral who, a thousand years before, had held a lily in front of his eyes when handing a towel to some naked bathers. In the afternoon they went to galleries. After tea they studied languages, usually helped by Mariana, the younger of Browning's two sisters, who spoke French and German fluently and was soon to open her own academy. Thus they passed the spring and summer. They returned home at the end of July, to coincide with the start of the summer holidays.

Apart from giving these useful insights, Barnes's letters were not very good, rather prosaic and unimaginative. He seems to have been a homely boy who was perfectly nice but a bit of a muff. Browning, however, clearly admired him, and so also, did Browning's mother; indeed from letters both of them sent to Mrs Barnes by way of reports, he appears to have been an ideal pupil, the child that every parent desired.

The boys who had stayed behind at Eton, those who had been in Browning's house who had had to move to other Tutors, and those who had boarded at other houses but, like Curzon, had been his pupils, all missed Browning acutely. In the first weeks of the spring half, in February 1876, as they saw his horses taken away, observed his carriages sent to auction, learnt that his boat and beloved canoe had been sold to another member of the staff, witnessed the carts remove his furniture, and said goodbye to his mother and sisters as all three set off for Germany to join his tutorial party at Leipzig, they felt a depth of genuine sorrow which boyish exuberance could not assuage and the daily lessons could not obliterate.

Many of them sent him long letters. 'Altogether I miss you DREADFULLY', wrote Oliver Vassall, one of his pupils, who at the age of nineteen, on the brink of a long and holy life – he became a celebrated Catholic priest – in a certain way took Browning's place, becoming the centre of a Browning group which contained Curzon and many others. He spoke for them all when he told Browning in an agitated letter of twelve pages that to say what Eton was like without him, to describe how much they were all missing him, was plainly and simply 'quite impossible'.

As well as the boys who were still at Eton, others wrote from Oxford and Cambridge, well understanding the intense bitterness from which Browning showed he was suffering; how he felt, as he wrote to one of them, 'ruined and disgraced'. Their letters reveal the true sympathy that only goes with genuine friendship, attachments that often lasted for life, as in the case of Frank Money whose name appeared with Gerald Balfour's in the Simeon Solomon correspondence. He was always 'your ever loving Frank', and addressed Browning like the poet that he was to become as 'dear, dear Beautifier of my days'.

Parents, too, wrote to commiserate; among others, Lord Portsmouth who still had two sons at Eton, and who had proved himself a genuine friend. Browning had often stayed at Eggesford, the Portsmouth mansion in North Devon, and had got to know the family well. His sons, Lord Portsmouth assured Browning, would ever look back with real affection on the homelike atmosphere of Browning's house, and would recollect for the rest of their lives with a sense of true gratitude and pleasure the happy, industrious time they had spent there. His youngest son, Frederic Henry who was then aged only six, 'your little friend Freddy Wallop', also wrote a charming letter to acknowledge with childish delight and gravity a present Browning had recently sent him.

Also, of course, his colleagues wrote, especially Luxmoore, Ainger and Cornish, all of whom had resigned in sympathy when Browning had first received his dismissal. They had only changed their minds and remained when they learnt that Browning's case was hopeless, that absolutely nothing could be done except provide him with abundant sympathy. So they wrote whenever they could to keep him abreast of all the news, especially news of his favourite pupils. 'Since you left', wrote Blanche Cornish, 'Eton has literally become a grave.' Yet, of course, as the months passed, as his house was taken over and filled, as his boys left and others arrived to whom his name was only a joke, the effect of his influence steadily diminished.

Soon athletics took over completely. In the years that followed, the duels at Lord's, the titanic struggles of the eights at Henley, became the boys' absorbing passions; and those who wished to roam the Brocas collecting butterflies like George Barnes, or writing poetry like Frank Money, found their interests hard to pursue. The giants of Pop and the captains of houses considered them proof of moral weakness. Games and sports became compulsory; and it soon grew to be an accepted dogma that a boy's morals as well as his muscles were all the better for constant exercise. Games promoted health and fatigue. Fatigue took care of 'wandering thoughts'. A boy who had rushed about all day had only one desire at night: to go to bed and fall asleep. He had no energy left for impure activities.

When Curzon left, two years later, covered with every Etonian glory – Captain of the Oppidans, Captain of his house, a member of Pop and multiple prizewinner – Browning effectively vanished from Eton. For just one flickering moment, in the winter of 1877, he became again the subject of gossip when, careless of Hornby's opinion and with Lord Scarsdale's entire approval, he went abroad with Curzon for the holidays. In a long, heartfelt, introspective letter, Curzon wrote to him on his return,[3]

'Ruined and disgraced'

My dear Mr. Browning

I must first thank you for the delightful little pencil case that arrived from London today with the equally delightful inscription on it – it now hangs at my watch chain & cannot fail whenever I use it to remind me of the tour which I am constantly looking back upon with feelings of the greatest pleasure and gratitude. I say gratitude, meaning to you, for since I have left you & more especially since my return here, I have felt how good and great an influence yours has been upon me during the last 3 weeks. You don't know how grateful I feel to you as I write this. Either the force of your own true example, or the teaching of your own pure doctrines has given me, I feel it, a seriousness I very much lacked before & which I very much need if ever I am to do anything in the world. The existence of this new feeling in me has been brought before me by events connected with this house which have occurred since my return – I heard evil things about it, and undoubtedly true ones – and I know the quick straight line I have taken would satisfy you. I recognise, more fully than I ever did before our recent conversations, the enormous responsibility that rests on the Captain of a House, and I see that while the mechanical duties of such a post have met with their due attention at my hands, there are other and more serious obligations of which I have not taken note. I thank you most deeply for awakening in me this better and more sensible feeling. You have made me feel too how much I need a well regulated mind & how poor a figure I cut in comparison with those who have it. I trust that knowing my deficiency, I may not belie my resolutions of trying to remedy it. Further I must thank you and this most of all for your trust in me. It is something to think that amidst an uncertain and disparaging surrounding of so-called friends, one has a true one to give the lie to their insinuations (true also though they sometimes be) and say a word for the sincerity which they sometimes unjustifiably impeach.

Your letter was such a delight to me. We were very great friends before our tour – but if I may say so, we are still greater now; and the absence from your society short though it has been has shewn me how much I value it. It was a cruel contrast exchanging your genial confidence for the dissatisfied and suspecting reception accorded to me by Stone: [his tutor] and I am afraid I don't like the man. The masters here are full of inquisitiveness about our tour and beset me with questions. Jock is well & sends you his love. He is a good friend also. You may be pleased to hear that I have won the Holiday Task Prize (for the 3rd time). Horngog is mild and apologetic. Dod bluff and good-humoured. Stone querulous and doubting. Myself your most affec friend, George N. Curzon

Curzon's letter was written to Cambridge, where Browning had retired, claiming his right as a Fellow of King's, under the statute of Henry VI, to devote the rest of his life to study there. His career at Eton was now over, Curzon's letter its simple epitaph. The first shock of bitterness had waned and he had reached the age of forty-one. A new, fruitful, industrious life lay, he believed, ahead of him.

CHAPTER VII

Colleagues, clubs,
and Sunday 'sociables'

Oscar Browning's cheerful arrival at King's in September 1876, a year almost to the day, since he had been dismissed from Eton, was not hailed with quite the delight that he liked to boast of in after years. True, champagne was drunk in Hall, and all but the Provost, Dr Okes, clasped his hand and greeted him warmly. Yet, behind the scenes there were doubts.

The College was a small, closed community with only a handful of resident Fellows who kept its affairs to themselves, entertained each other in the evenings, and had no desire to welcome newcomers. Any arrival was bound to upset them. Browning's appearance, with his reputation as an extremely difficult colleague – worst of all a 'violent reformer' – caused them the greatest anxiety.

Already, long before he had reached them, he had made an undesirable disturbance, having his rooms completely refurbished in a rather modern and *outré* manner: with Turkey carpets, Morris wallpapers and several miles of oak shelving. His furniture had arrived in huge vans which had jammed the entrance to King's Parade; and his books, of which there were seven thousand, had blocked the staircase to his rooms for weeks. During the summer when he was abroad, reports had reached them of long diatribes, given to every passing tourist, in every hotel and club he visited, criticising Eton and everything to do with it. Since the Fellows were all Etonians, all acquainted with Goodford and Hornby, they had followed Browning's dismissal minutely, and few, if any, thought him blameless. His prodigal's return to King's afterwards, whatever his rights and qualifications, and in spite of polite murmurs to the contrary, filled many with dismay.

He was perfectly aware of his colleagues' mistrust and of the only way to allay it. He had to control his restless, provoking manner, and, by a solid piece of work, thoroughly researched and soundly written, to claim their respect as a serious historian. He was fully determined to start at once, and confided his resolves to his mother and friends: to rise early and work methodically, to live simply and inexpensively, to renounce self and material gain, to work only for the good of the college. It is sad, with the benefit of after-knowledge, to see how few, if any, of these goals he achieved.

It was not for want of friendly warnings. In particular James Welldon gave him the frankest possible advice. An Eton pupil and now a Scholar at King's, Welldon, like Curzon, was destined to justify Browning's predictions and achieve many notable distinctions. In a letter written before Browning arrived, in June 1876, he warned him with almost religious solemnity of the dangers and difficulties that lay before him.[1]

> Honestly and sincerely I feel that you have a difficult task before you at King's; not less honestly and sincerely I say to you that, if you act wisely, you may, I believe, do a great and useful work there. You know as well as I do that, when you first come to Cambridge you will find yourself regarded by the majority of King'smen with a considerable amount of suspicion; even those who rank among your friends are fearful lest you should, by injudicious interference, make the business and management of the College less pleasant than it might be. That suspicion it will be your first object to dispel. As long as people distrust you, as long as they think that you are actuated by mere love of meddling, by a wish to be prominent or by any other motive than a simple sense of duty, your usefulness must be impaired. On this account it will assuredly be your duty to avoid offending the feelings of those among whom you live. If you are always abusing King's, if you constantly institute comparisons between King's and Trinity to the discredit of the former, nay even if within the College itself you are too forward in pushing Reform which must come sooner or later, and for which I am no less anxious than yourself you will certainly excite an amount of ill feeling which will be injurious to the best interests of King's and very prejudicial to your own influence . . . All I can say to you is that you will require great tact

in dealing with the members, particularly the older members of the College. Not less tact will you need in your relations to undergraduates generally. I don't doubt that, whatever be your line of action, you will be able to gather round you a large number of undergraduate friends. But if your wish is, as I understand, to do good more especially to King's, to promote among the young members of your College a real living sympathy with all that is highest and noblest in literature and in conduct, then your task will be more difficult. You will have, as it were, to sink your apostleship without for one moment ceasing to be and to act as an Apostle; you will have to win the confidence of some among the undergraduates without giving offence to others – for to split up the College into two strongly opposed factions is in itself undesirable and will certainly mar the good effect of your influence – above all you will have to appreciate what is good in King's itself, whilst all the while you are trying to make that good better. And in all this you will be helped more than I can tell you by doing that which is so clearly before your eyes, by leading a truly 'simple and laborious life', by 'doing away entirely with the notion of gain' or of any self-advancement, by 'devoting yourself entirely to the service of the College and of the University', in short by quite forgetting self . . . I am especially glad that you propose to aid in establishing a school of history and political philosophy for that is, I think, your forte – to work for the College so far as you can do so 'without interfering with other people' particularly Prothero who is likely to be most useful at King's and to help forward the great work of improving the education of women. Indeed I know not how anyone can desire a wider sphere of usefulness than will be open to you.

Prothero, mentioned in Welldon's letter, was a Fellow of King's and Lecturer in History, a subject only lately recognised as worthy of serious consideration. He was Browning's junior by eleven years, and thus, as a younger member of the College, more ready to welcome Browning with greater sincerity than many others. 'I am honestly glad you are coming', he said, writing to Browning before he arrived, revealing, *en passant*, a cheerful snobbishness, characteristic of King's at the time. He was, he explained, away in Nottingham, lecturing to what he called the 'Provincial Cad'. He thought Browning should lecture on Treaties in the second half of the eighteenth century; not entirely a suitable subject for anyone like Browning who hated compromise.

Browning's immediate problem was money – he got none officially for giving lectures, either from King's or the University; his only income came from his Fellowship, yearly a mere £300, exactly a tenth of his income at Eton. To give him a start, a group of friends under the aegis of John Seeley, Regius Professor of Modern History, most generously subscribed a fund from which annually, for three years, he received £150. There had been a plan to endow a Lectureship to which he would then have been appointed, but the old guard at King's prevented it. For what were really obvious reasons, they felt that a gift of this description could not be accepted with any condition that Browning should be its first recipient.

Another proposal to augment his income – as important for the status it would confer as for the augmentation of income – was to elect him College Tutor. Again, the old guard prevented it. Austen Leigh, the retiring Tutor and newly elected Vice Provost, advised him frankly in a long letter that, for the now familiar reasons – his reputation for being contentious – he, at least, would never vote for him.[2]

> The question is as to your qualifications for this special post. I believe that you would attract people to the College; but I also think (though I did not say this last night) that you wd. prevent others from coming. This wd. be chiefly the case with those Eton boys whose parents or Tutors consider you a dangerous person; but I suspect that the strong feeling both for you & against you extends beyond Eton.
>
> If it were a mere question of *numbers*, I dare say your admirers would provide us with larger entries than we shd. otherwise get: what I fear is that the College wd. get to be a College of a particular party & this wd., I believe, be bad for it in the long run.
>
> In saying this, I am of course paying a compliment to your vigour & power of influencing others, which I feel to be far beyond mine. You could not be a Tutor here, without being *the* prominent one. Of course I am aware that, having this opinion of your powers

& yet declining to vote for you, I might be thought to be jealous of you. Perhaps the best answer that I could make to any such suspicion would be to say what is the simple truth, viz: that I fully intend to retire altogether from the office of Tutor as soon as I think I can do so without injuring the College.

I also said last night that I thought that you were actually deficient in some qualities which seem to me essential for a Tutor. It seems to me that your judgement & discretion are not equal to your energy, enthusiasm, & power of work. I am quite aware that I cannot *prove* this; I can only say that such is the conviction in my mind, & that I must be guided by it.

Browning, therefore, remained isolated, a resident Fellow without status, having only permission to lecture, the use of a room in which to do so, and such fees from such pupils as his course on Treaties managed to attract.

He wrote cheerfully back to his mother that the College had made him a 'local centre', that all his hopes were being fulfilled. To others who knew the actual truth like his old friend Francis Hodgson with whom he had been in College at Eton and to whom he wrote a long letter, he did not attempt to conceal his disappointment.

If, however, his colleagues rejected him, the undergraduates welcomed him at once. Within a month of returning to Cambridge, in October 1876, he formed a discussion group for historians, all of whom were undergraduates – no dons were allowed but himself – which he called the Political Society. This club which flourishes today, now entitled the Historical Society, met in his rooms on Monday evenings. It was limited, at first, to a membership of twelve who, in the manner of the Trinity 'Apostles' whose customs, in fact, they largely followed, drew counters from a velvet bag (still a prized relic at King's) to decide the order in which they would speak.[3] The proceedings began at nine o'clock with cups of tea and ginger biscuits; at nine-thirty a paper was read, the essayist holding forth from the hearthrug; discussion followed, and then a vote; at ten-thirty the evening ended. O.B. as Browning was called (at Cambridge everyone used his initials except his colleagues on formal occasions) reposed by the fire in an armchair, covering his face with a red bandana. Even his most devoted admirers had to admit that on certain occasions he definitely fell asleep.

The debates, however, were often stimulating. O.B. opened the first, reading an essay on modern Russia, and posing the question, still so relevant, 'Should we fear the hug of the Russian Bear?' The motion was negatived by four to one, O.B. voting with the 'Noes'. By this essay the tone was set: 'Is war necessary to the progress of civilisation?' 'Was Cromwell a Creator or a Creature of History?' Another question put was: 'Is it desirable that the present view of private property in land should be retained?'

The 'Noes' won in this discussion, among their number being Austen Chamberlain. Severe shock was felt by the secretary at this attack on the landed establishment. He felt obliged to note in the minutes, 'The Society proved itself to be revolutionary by 8 to 1.' The Society also proved to be anti-imperial. It voted 'no' to the following proposal, again with the help of Austen Chamberlain. 'Is it desirable that England should remain an Empire?' O.B. was deeply alarmed, and tried to upset the result by voting twice.

Frivolity sometimes reared its head. 'Were there party distinctions before the Flood?' was asked by a speaker, Leo Maxse. No decision was reached that evening. In November 1885, at the 138th meeting a paper was read that was so boring that all who heard it collapsed in sleep. The offending essayist was P.H. Sturge who drugged his friends with a dusty document, 'Contemporary Whig opinion of the Treaty of Utrecht'.

The form of the motion is not recorded, but to make a change and revive the proceedings, the house divided into 'Port' or 'Claret' instead of the customary 'Ayes' or 'Noes'. The latter triumphed by four to three, but the margin apparently should have been larger as one of the participants, Townsend-Warner, still obviously fuddled by the Treaty, voted for 'Port' when he meant, he said, to have voted, in fact, for 'Claret'.

Looking seriously at this Society of which O.B. was justly

proud, and over which without a break, he presided for more than thirty years, it is clear that it provided for a real need. All students in the complex fields of history and politics look for informal, exploratory guidance. For O.B. the need was as great: that continual hunger felt by all teachers for receptive students to whom to offer their views and experience. In O.B.'s case it was the comparative few who as statesmen or civil servants would soon be governing the British Empire. The ambition to mould the minds of the great, to rock the cradles of the sons of kings, was always a driving force behind his activities.

The Political Society was so successful that almost immediately he started others. Always passionately fond of music, he started a club for amateurs of Mozart which met in his rooms on Thursday evenings. He himself played the piano (he possessed a 'grand' as well as an 'upright'), weaving about on a stool like a seal, his fat fingers like flabby sticks, banging the notes with hideous consequences. The others brought their own instruments, and gave him as much support as they could. The ensuing noise was usually appalling, later on substantially increased by the introduction of orchestrinas. These mechanical miniature organs which made a series of whines and groans that represented stringed instruments, enormously increased the scope of the repertoire. After a while, O.B. had four. They were universally known as 'obeophones'. Their owner pronounced them 'awfully jolly', though the noise they made when played together, drove his neighbours nearly mad. Sometimes, however, professionals played; on one occasion, the great Joachim. Then his neighbours opened their doors.

Like everything else that O.B. did, his Musical Society was frequently ridiculed; yet, when his activities also concerned the young whose minds were open, he often touched a responsive chord which then led them on to higher things.

The unfortunate residents of Wilkins' Building were disturbed also on Sunday evenings. Shortly after he returned to Cambridge he started being 'at home' on Sundays, not only to members of his own College, whether dons or undergraduates, but to everyone else as well. After Hall, from nine to eleven, he received anyone who chose to visit. Into the entrance to 'A' staircase, round the elegant gothic balusters, up the forty-six steps, under the coved and plastered ceiling, and through the fluted, mediaeval doors came colleagues, pupils, friends and strangers from every corner of the university. There, before them in spacious rooms, lined from floor to ceiling with books, and filled with pictures, clocks and knick-knacks they found a portly, mincing host never failing to be pleased to see them. The air was soon thick with smoke, and every chair and settee occupied. In the then extremely bohemian fashion, later arrivals sat on the floor. Some talked, a few sang, others strummed the grand piano. Conversation and whisky warmed them. By ten o'clock, if not before, the noise was positively indescribable.

O.B.'s 'perpendiculars' became a feature of the university, and for thirty years no one had arrived until they had been to one of his 'sociables'. They were half a joke and half an institution – and very useful. Generations of undergraduates have described how, when they went, their eyes were opened for the first time to whole vistas of the adult world the like of which they had never imagined. Desmond MacCarthy is a good example. Although at King's years afterwards, in the first decade of the twentieth century, the scene he described had remained unchanged.[4]

O.B.'s at homes (Sunday evenings) were amazing affairs, and the first one I attended, soon after coming up, was something of a shock to me, aged seventeen. Entering, I caught straight in the face a blast of native air from off the heights of Intellectual Bohemia, a country of which I was to become a denizen. I sniffed; I did not like it. It made me cough, a cough of bewildered decorum. Imagine two large rooms lined nearly to the ceiling with dusky undusted books (there must have been about ten thousand of them), and with a little bedroom beyond, of which guests were equally free; big tables with a school-feast litter of cups and cake on them, syphons, whisky bottles, glasses, urns, jugs of lemonade; the air blue with tobacco smoke; a great hum of conversation – though quite a number of men were standing about not talking to anyone. Such an aquarium of strange people I had never yet seen. In one corner a man, whom I recognised as a famous metaphysician, was being badgered by a couple of undergraduates, 'What did he, what could *anyone* mean by the Unity of Apperception?' In an armchair an elderly peer, who had evidently enjoyed the College wine in the Common Room, was slowly expounding politics, with the help of a cigar, to a circle of squatting young men; standing by the fire a Tommy in scarlet uniform was shaking into the flames the spittle from the clarinet he had just ceased playing; here and there, seated on the floor, were pairs of friends conversing earnestly in low tones as oblivious as lovers of their surroundings . . . Presently the piano began in the room beyond, and we went in to watch our host trolling out *Voi che sapete* with immense gusto. At the close of his performance the clarinet-player gave him a spanking, which I thought a most undignified incident.

At these parties the undergraduates encountered life, for O.B.'s acquaintanceship was wide, and from every class and corner of society. Then, of course, also they met one another. To arrange to meet at O.B.'s rooms was a normal, popular, convenient arrangement. A tryst on 'A' staircase might lead to a stroll through a college court; and later on, a touch of the hand, in the cool, green, shining Cambridge meadows.

In just such a green meadow in the spring of 1878 a handsome, athletic, clever boy, one of O.B.'s Eton pupils, had unsuspectingly formed a friendship which had led to tragic circumstances. The precise details are not clear, but evidently the boy, James Wilson, eldest son of a Welsh clergyman, at the time an undergraduate of Trinity, had formed an attachment for another man which had not been wholly reciprocated. To James Wilson's intense shame his love had somehow been discovered. On a Saturday evening at the end of May, on his way to visit friends at Eton, he had put a dramatic end to his life by walking in front of a locomotive.

This drama epitomised for some the profound need to recognise the innocence of homosexual love, a recognition passionately sought by many intelligent, sensitive men, one leader amongst whom was J.A. Symonds. O.B. knew Symonds well, having met him years before in Dresden, and always kept up with him. At the end of the term he wrote to Symonds and told him the whole, unhappy story. Symonds was genuinely, deeply moved, and out of sympathy wrote a poem.[5]

A tragedy of our days

He loved, & thought no shame;
But spake divinely bold;
Simple & void of blame
As were the Greeks of old.

Yet on his lip was death:
For when he spake, the word
Winged by that fervent breath
A thundrous echo stirred.

He therefore, late made wise,
Went forth & nothing said,
With clear and candid eyes,
Although his heart was dead.

Too pure to brook a stain,
Too proud his wound to hide,
Under the rushing train
He laid him down and died.

O.B.'s activities at King's which either disturbed or annoyed his colleagues were not confined to the undergraduates. King's was undergoing reform, being required by an Act of Parliament – as were other colleges at Cambridge – to provide itself with new statutes. Meetings were held almost weekly. O.B. always attended them. His love of debate and blind conviction that whatever he proposed must be the best, drove his colleagues close to total distraction.

The basic question before the Fellows was how the College ought to be managed. It was still controlled, in effect, by the Provost, as in the days of Henry VI, 430 years earlier. Dr Okes, the reigning incumbent, had reached the venerable age of eighty, and although loved and much respected, he had lost the reforming vigour of his youth, and found it easier to rule by veto. Also he lived in a large Lodge in grounds that were badly needed, and enjoyed a salary far greater – seven times more than a Fellow's – than his duties or style as Provost required. O.B. approached this problem, and the several others to which it was allied, with common sense but a lack of diplomacy, setting out his views in a pamphlet[6] with all the concealed edge of criticism so easily attached to the written word. He proposed that under the revised statutes, the Provost's successor ought to be elected; that he ought to occupy a smaller Lodge; that his salary ought to be greatly reduced; that his term should be limited to ten years. These ideas were all good, and in later years, many were adopted. Yet at the time, they gave extreme offence to many of his colleagues.

In his private life a personal sorrow disturbed the year of his return to Cambridge. In December 1878, George Eliot's husband died. O.B. wrote her the following letter.[7]

My dear Mrs Lewes

I hope that I shall not be intrusive in writing to tell you with what a terrible shock the news fell upon me on Tuesday morning that your husband was dead. I had the liveliest remembrance of that bright brilliant evening we spent together at the Halls, of his speech after dinner & of that delightful talk afterwards, when he and Tourgenieff were a worthy match. My first feeling was for you, and for the desolation which I know you must feel who had been accustomed to lean so completely on his perfect love – my next for him in his unfinished work, and the pang of parting from and leaving you alone. Still you have those years of absolute trust & affection to look back to.

Forgive me if I have said too much. Your friendship and his have been too dear to me for me to have said less. Do not trouble to answer this. I am sure to hear of you from some common friends.

Believe me, Yrs very sincerely, Oscar Browning.

He never saw George Eliot again, although it was thought by some that he wanted to marry her. His social life in Cambridge and London, his private literary projects and lectures, his travels abroad with undergraduates, completely absorbed his time and energies. Whether he loved George Eliot or not, he had no real desire for marriage with her or anybody else.

In the course of 1878 he went, as usual, to Italy and Germany, spent a month with friends in Scotland, and travelled constantly up to London to take part in social and musical festivities. Always collecting the great and the famous, but distinguished enough himself, too, to attract lions to his own receptions, he entertained them whenever he could. His guests included William Gladstone, Robert Browning, William Morris, and a host of other stars and satellites in political, social and artistic life whose names he joyfully recorded in his diary.

How he ever did any work remained a mystery to all his colleagues, especially those on 'A' staircase whose own tranquil entertainments scarcely ruffled the calm of King's from one year's beginning to the next. When he offered to coach some students for their Indian Civil Service examinations – for him an extra-curricular burden – their tutor, Hammond, a Fellow of Trinity, felt obliged to voice his objections. 'I don't think any man in the world could do really well so many things as you think of undertaking . . . the history men can't do without the best lectures in Pol. Phil. which you can produce. But I know you have a power of doing several things immediately along side of one another which is unknown to me.'[8]

This power he possessed to a fault. From the very day he returned to King's, it directly caused him much unhappiness. His ability to juggle with all his interests and to keep them all on the go at a time, always provoked his colleagues' annoyance. Also, it stopped him doing any work of more than a clever, superficial character. He meant, as he often told his mother, to write a history of George I; a solid work of real value by which he hoped to make his name. His gregarious instincts proved too strong. He could never settle to the long haul which any *magnum opus* requires. Love of youth and conversation forever took him away from the task. After a few years at Cambridge, much to his mother's profound disappointment and much to his own uneasy surprise, a quite different reputation began to develop around him.

CHAPTER VIII

The patron of youth

O.B.'s dismissal from Eton from which he thought he would never recover, in some respects proved a blessing in disguise. For the very first time in his life, at the full age of forty-one, he was free to do exactly as he pleased without having to consult his mother. Although he missed her presence continually, and wrote to her regularly every week with a detailed account of most of his doings, his private life was able to expand in a manner previously quite impossible. Not only had he time to be sociable, but time also to devote to youth – to do so how and where he pleased, and in ways which before had necessarily been kept in check by being an Eton schoolmaster.

In this field his avuncular interests – for often they were simply these, nothing more than a sentimental wish to please a boy with a pretty face, perhaps to give him an enormous tea or a few shillings for a new fishing rod – often caused him a lot of trouble.

One summer he gave a tip to one of the College Chapel choristers. The boy had demonstrated the Chapel organ for the benefit of one of O.B.'s friends, for which he had pocketed half-a-crown. Nixon, the Dean, came to hear of it and ordered the boy to return the money. To dally with the dons or accept presents, also of course to meddle with the organ, was strictly against the choir-school rules. Naturally O.B. knew this well, but characteristically felt offended when Nixon politely gave him a rebuke.

Then followed, almost inevitably, an acrimonious passage of arms of the kind O.B. so much enjoyed. He wrote immediately to Nixon twice, two letters on the same day, although Nixon lived next door, in the same building on 'D' staircase. Nixon felt obliged to reply. He received a retort within the hour. O.B.'s explanations developed and became personal and more specious. Finally, as almost always happened with anyone trying to persuade O.B. that anything he said was not quite true, or anything he did was not correct, Nixon decided not to continue. 'Dear Browning', he wrote in conclusion, his script getting smaller and smaller, and less and less neat and horizontal as he neared the bottom of the fourth page of what was then his third letter,[1]

> I have no recollection of having as Dean given prizes or presents without the cognizance of the College or the Headmaster nor of having broken the rule at the time when I had ceased to be Dean. Consequently your reference (*without explanation*) to your 'suggestion that I might sometime in the kindness of my heart have given presents to Choristers' seems to me at least gratuitous, if not what some would call, an impertinently fishing enquiry, which on principle I should have declined to notice but I had to choose between the loss of dignity, if you can understand this, and the risk of misinterpretation. You will I hope see in this a fresh reason for discontinuing the correspondence as our views about propriety in correspondence are clearly divergent.
> Yours truly, J.E. Nixon
>
> [August 15th 1888]

O.B., as usual, took no notice. He had often given presents to choristers, quite harmlessly in his opinion. He had sometimes got to know them well. More than once a friendship had blossomed which had proved of mutual benefit. He was, in fact, at that moment reaping a very positive reward for having befriended another chorister by the name of Charlie Copeman.

He had known Charlie for several years, and had not merely given him money but everything from suits to hampers of food, his father being a penniless Canon with four other sons to educate. After Charlie had left the Choir School, O.B. had kept in touch with him, had helped him through his next school, and had managed to finance his return to Cambridge with an annual allowance of one hundred pounds. He was now at Selwyn and doing well. This success, O.B. considered, fully justified all his efforts to keep in touch with promising boys, especially those in need of help, whether in the choir or anywhere else, and simply proved, if proof were needed, that Nixon's strictures were absurd.

Of course, O.B. had fallen for Charlie. He had taken him swimming, paid for his photograph, had him to stay for weekends at King's, and doubtless given him prurient embraces. He had even written about him to Symonds who had generously sent him £15. O.B.'s letter to Symonds has vanished, but the latter's reply reveals its tenor. He asked if Charlie would like to stay with him, and begged O.B. to send him a photograph. 'I only wish', he concluded fervently, 'that I had the privilege of calling that young gentleman my friend.'[2]

If Charlie had caused O.B. any trouble, it was only in answering his weekly letters. Charlie had written every Sunday for all the years he had been at school – more than two hundred letters. O.B. must have wished at times that Charlie's devotional flame would subside, for if he failed to answer at once, he received a further, urgent epistle in which he was tearfully begged to reply. He was writing, too, every week to Charlie's younger brother, Alfred, a pupil at King's School, Peterborough. Alfred, however, had started to bore him. 'I wish you would write me a few lines in your own handwriting', Alfred complained. 'I wish you would write to me *once* yourself. It doesn't seem as if you like me any longer, always to write through your amanuensis . . .' 'You never write to me now . . . I hope you will write. With love, I remain ever your affectionate little friend . . .'[3]

Alfred was nearly seventeen, too old to be sweet, whatever he wrote. Charlie, however, remained in favour. He took his degree and became a solicitor. Whatever the friendship may have cost in terms of time or trouble or expense, it more than paid for itself for both. It gave Charlie the chance to get on, and it gave O.B. a patron's pleasure, the first recorded in his Cambridge life of his many philanthropic successes.

A failure, however was in the offing. In the spring of 1889, O.B. went to the Isle of Wight taking with him a lad called Matthew Oates. Oates was a poor boy from Cambridge, newly apprenticed 'before the mast' to the Shaw Savill shipping line, the first of many of O.B.'s protégés to join the Royal or Merchant Navy. O.B. took him to Robbie Ross, the friend and executor of Oscar Wilde, then an undergraduate at King's who was also visiting the island. Ross thought him quite delightful, 'very beautiful and very charming'. (Ross had just been ducked at King's for his long hair and aesthetic mannerisms.) Both men spoilt and petted him. Such behaviour went to Oates's head, and led to predictably tiresome consequences.

On his first voyage he was sent to New Zealand, but once there he jumped ship. After a few exciting days of complete freedom in a strange land, he ran out of money and gave himself up. To break indentures was a serious offence, and he only got himself out of trouble, and a passage home at the Company's expense, by using O.B.'s name as a reference. He sailed, next, to North America. Here he jumped ship again, and the Company firmly told O.B. who had stood by him until then that no further employment was possible. Oates, however, was unabashed, and wrote O.B. a familiar letter.[4]

> Tacoma
> Wash.
> November 25th
>
> Dear Old Chap
>
> Just a line to tell you I have not ceased to live. I am getting along famous with everybody as yet. Tacoma is a very nice place but very dull. There is plenty of Squars here ugly old cows, I do not have any thing to do with them I am turned for the better now I am quite modist. I want you to get me a ship when I come home I will not make an ass of you this time. Get me a ship if you can thers a brick. I have not much new to tell you now will tell all when I come home so good bye.
>
> I remain, Yours ever faithfully, M.J. Oates

Clearly at one time in the past, sex had crept into their relationship.

His mother, knowing nothing of this, thanked O.B. from the bottom of her heart for all he had tried to do for her son. 'Words cannot express how much I thank you for your great kindness to

Matt. It will never lay in my power to reward you on earth but God I know will fully do it, if not here in the next world . . .'

This sincere and appreciative letter, the last in a file of nearly fifty, proved to be O.B.'s only reward for what, in spite of indiscretions, had been a well-intentioned effort to improve the lot of a penniless youngster. Later, Oates came to London, and used O.B. as a reference again. He rented a room in Pall Mall, and then disappeared without paying for it. He stole the key, which was almost worse, as the room could not be re-let without it. Miss Higgs whose house it was, asked O.B. to help her trace him. She wrote twice but got no reply. By then O.B. must have made up his mind that the 'Fair Sailor' as Ross called him had best be allowed to go back to the sea and vanish.

Yet, in spite of the failure with Oates, the time wasted with the Copeman family, or the row with Nixon over the chorister, nothing stopped him collecting boys whose manners he liked or whose faces pleased him. Quite regardless of any of the risks, especially of blackmail and venereal disease – and there were signs in later life that his lusts had given him medical problems – he never paused to reckon the cost. If a clever, handsome or cheerful youth ever appeared in need of assistance, O.B.'s heart was immediately stirred, and he thought simply of trying to find a way to help him. Only afterwards, in some cases, did other activities arise.

Most of the boys he set his eyes on came from Cambridge or round about, the sons of tradesmen or local farmers. Quite a number were 'boy sailors' (the Navy League had a branch in Cambridge). Others came from the great Nowhere, picked literally from off the streets. John Sheppard, Fellow of King's, in a journal now in the College Library, tells of one who came from Cambridge, found destitute on Parker's Piece. O.B.'s nephew, Wortham, speaks of another, rescued starving from a Paris boulevard.

These boys came to his rooms and, according to their different needs, were given food, clothing or money; often, too, an exciting bath. O.B.'s rooms were the first in College to have a private bath en-suite. Later on he found them employment. All that he usually asked in return was that those who could from time to time, should write and tell him how they managed to get on.

In fact, a great many of them did so. From these letters much can be told, not only of how they fared thereafter on land, sea and in the brothel, but also of how O.B. had treated them. His files bulge with their cheerful reports. Even before the days of his fame, when his reputation as a friend of youth had become established in the Cambridge district and caused an endless flow of enquiries from boys themselves as well as their parents, his 'AMBERG'S patent indexed cabinet' in which he tucked their appealing missives, often looked as though it would burst. One letter led to another; and if a lad got into trouble, fell in love, or needed money, then the letters arrived in shoals.

Soon these defaulters lost their charm, and O.B. did his best to get rid of them. Sometimes, if ignored, they wrote to him even more than before. At times they must have been really troublesome. Yet O.B. was never dismayed, and never appeared to have any regrets. As one chum became a nuisance, he found another to take his place. Whether from kindness, love, or lust, he simply could not resist another engagement.

The sailors gave him the most amusement. His nephew Wortham, in his biography, describes how O.B. used to treat them – how he used to visit their ships, give them teas and send them hampers. Wortham did not refer to their letters. Probably he never read them. Albert Brown wrote from Devonport:[5]

I went ashore here last sunday with some more boys and we did have a lovely time. We went into a shop called the change up stairs and laid down a six penny piece and asked for a penny worth of sweets so being on for a bit of fun I said to the woman I will have the change up stairs so she said walk this way and I and a chum went into a side room and there were to nice girls waiting for us so we picked one apeice and we were all right I can tell you so after we had done we came out and off we went on board so that was a cheap cut but I felt dead off in the morning.

> I remain, your affectionate, old friend, A.E. Brown
> write back quick and let me know the news
> how did the boy treat you allright like me

The patron of youth

Later, Albert wrote from China:

I have just had a look at your photo you know that is all I have to
remember you. I should love to have a little thing belonging to you
for a keep sake as most of your friends have something to remember
you as you are so kind to us blue jackets so I think you might send
me a small keepsake one that I should pride. Your photo I have in a
little frame in my ditty box on the lid so when I open my box theres
your face looking at me . . .

Stanley Chivers, O.B.'s valet, also later joined the Navy.
Known to his friends as the 'imp of Satan' he wrote to O.B. after
he had left him.[6]

You may think I'm a silly fool for leaving England but I have
always wanted to go to sea & so now I have the oppo I mean to go.
Believe me I am very grateful for all your past kindness I know now
what a little beast you must have thought me abroad. [Eventually, he reached Yokohama.] I hope you are enjoying good
health. I am in splendid condition. I went ashore last Sunday &
enjoyed myself thoroughly. I visited the skivy houses & had a short
time price, 1 dollar, 2/6.

Charlie Fox, another valet who, like Chivers, left for the Navy,
sent O.B. the news from Hamburg.[7] 'Dear Sir. I must tell you
how awfully good I have been since I left home. I have actually
only slept with one girl, and she was a regular tip topper . . . I
hope you are well & flourishing as usual. I remain, dear Sir,
Your Sincere Friend, Charlie.'

Frederick Brand, wanting money for a girl he had got in the
family way, wrote on paper embossed with forget-me-nots,
and sent O.B. a mass of kisses.[8] 'Kind Sir. I am writing to ask
you to do me a favour by lending me £2 until the 1st of January
for I've got into a bother ashore with a young lady and if you
could be a friend to me now you will be a friend inneed. Dear Sir
I dont want you to think that I want you to give me the money
but to lend me it I will repay you as soon as possible. I am yours
in waiting Fred your Sailor Boy. XXXXXX'

Robert Anderson, another valet, joined the Army and went to India. 'You always used to tell me to tell you all my secrets', he wrote.[9] Of the natives he reported, 'You ask me which I find the most fascinating, Black or White, the latter, most decidedly the latter, there's nothing in the former in my eye.' When he came home he got into trouble. 'You are the only friend I have in the world', he wrote, asking for money. O.B. sent him £5. He married, had children, and afterwards deserted them. Then O.B. had letters from his wife. Their number rose to thirty-one before O.B. got bored and ceased to answer them.

There were also many ordinary letters, containing nothing but news and thanks, and without sex or complications. Albert Hyde, another sailor, wrote an almost endless series – over the years, more than one hundred – using romantic nautical paper, headed by a neat steel engraving of Jack Tar leaning on an anchor. George Chapman, another soldier, also had an innocent relationship. He thanked O.B. for a 'loving letter'. '. . . I am without a friend except you, kind Sir . . .' 'Please do write to me again, for your letters are so nice.' '. . . so I thank you for the many kind things you have done for me and if any time the mouse can help the lion, apply of your very thankfull George Chapman. Please write.'

Letters such as Hyde's and Chapman's which were all fun, innocence and gratitude, and of which there are more than a thousand, gave O.B. enormous pleasure.[10] He showed them off to acquaintances and colleagues. He sent some to a friend in the Admiralty who described their authors as 'our finest fellows'. He passed others to J.R. Selwyn, the Master of Selwyn College, Cambridge. 'My Dear Browning', the latter wrote, 'I return the letters which are quite delightful. While the Navy recruits such boys she will have good stuff in her as they grow up.'[11]

A crush on a boy called Percy Shelton produced an entirely different result. His father wrote, 'Many thanks for your kind enquiries & for your kindly interest in Percy. Since his visit to London in the spring he has shown an unreasonable spirit of indifference even to resentment for your sympathy which has been a trouble to both Mrs S. & myself.'[12] O.B. wrote back from his Sussex retreat:

> Dearest Percy, write I will
> From this lovely place, Bexhill.
> How I wish that you were here,
> With your eyes so pure and clear (!)
> And your merry little face,
> Laughing with a strange grimace
> And those ruddy little cheeks
> Which each passing feeling speaks.

He was not to be squashed as easily as that when so many other people admired him. Indeed, as he settled down at King's, and as, at last, his colleagues accepted him, ceased to look for works of scholarship, and shrugged him off as mildly eccentric, his reputation as a lover of boys almost assumed respectability. If he were not a Gibbon or Macaulay, the author of a great historical work, he was at least a personality, widely acclaimed as a patron of youth.

Consider the evidence. Look at the letters. A Cambridge boy, Frederick Kidman, aged eighteen, wanting work, wrote to him, '. . . knowing that you are a gentleman who are willing to help anyone . . .' A local tradesman, Francis Lyons, approached him on behalf of Spencer Pleasance, aged fifteen, 'a good willing boy'. 'Having heard of your kind interest in boys, I am venturing to appeal to you . . .'

A London waif, Samuel Leeland who washed railway carriages at King's Cross, begged O.B. for a pair of boots.[13] O.B. kindly sent him some money. 'I cant thank you enough for your great kindness to me I received the order quite safe I must again thank you very much Sir I will do all that you wish me to do to please you is more than all I have got in all the world Sir I must again thank thank you again a thousand times for what you have sent me . . .'

Lastly, a letter from a London draper:[14]

The patron of youth

Dear Mr. Browning

Now I think you are safely back in College therefore I will now do what I have long wanted, viz to thank you for your extreme kindness to my boy, for inasmuch as you have done it unto him, you have done it unto me, and I may say to his mother also, and I am well aware you are fond of boys and I think this quotation from the great man will strictly apply. 'May you long continue in favour with your colleagues, and when your bones have run their course and sleep in blessings, may they have a tomb of childrens tears wept on them.'

A very nice youth who has lived very close to me, is now at Trinity his name is Burlisson. I have told him to seek you, for I know you will advance him and perhaps be that sun that will usher forth his glories, and for him may that sun never set.

I know also that your kindness is not always appreciated, but I am quite sure that will not alter your set purpose to do good. And as a man's reputation is the immortal part of himself, so may it be said of you, although Dynasties have fallen and Empires crumbled into dust, the charity of Oscar Browning to the boys with whom he came into contact is imperishably written in the pages of Life's History. Hoping you are well.

Yours very sincerely, William Bacon

O.B. often used to remark, as many others had done before him, that when it came to being appreciated, little honour can be found at home. It had always been the same story. No one had understood him at Eton, and no one at Cambridge knew him now. By common consent, except at King's, in the world outside and the popular press, he was, by the time of Bacon's letter, one of the most successful dons in the University.

CHAPTER IX

The man of the day

O.B.'s view of his own importance was not conceit or hallu-
cination. In the 1890s, aged then in his middle fifties, and after
fifteen years at King's, he enjoyed the esteem of a large and
varied circle. As a popular tutor and teacher of history, he was
held in repute in his own profession; as the author of nearly
twenty books, he was widely read at home and abroad; as a
founder member of the Eighty Club, and a still aspiring parliamentary candidate, he was heard with respect in Liberal con-
claves; as a friend of dandies like Oscar Wilde, he had made a
niche in aesthetic society; as one of the greatest snobs in the
world, he was well known to, if not admired by every monarch,
prince and duke in Europe.

He was best known to the general public, the public who
never came to Cambridge, for his 'Lives' of famous literary
figures and his books and essays on European history. Apart
from some articles in the *Encyclopaedia Britannica*, two of which,
on Goethe and Dante, he later enlarged and published as books,
he had written very successful primers on Modern England and
Modern France; produced studies of mediaeval Italy; edited
numerous Foreign Office documents; written widely about
Napoleon; compiled a treatise on Citizens' Rights; composed a
Life of George Eliot; and sent to the press, in four volumes, *A
New Illustrated History of England*.

His style in all these different productions was light, clear and
unprofessorial, just what the general public liked. The fact that
he often made mistakes, that his sense of place was frequently
poor, that his dates were often absurdly wrong, he considered a
matter of no importance. Such things were easily corrected. If
Africa appeared instead of Asia, it was easy to sort them out on a
map. If 1609 became 1906 it was simple to switch the 9 and the
6. If, in the troubled history of Italy, a Guelph occasionally
became a Ghibelline, it was only a matter of changing them

over. When once challenged by a correspondent who pointed out this anomaly in his popular study *Guelphs and Ghibellines* (which he dedicated to J.A. Symonds), he defended himself with deft frivolity. His explanation was extremely neat. Quite obviously, in this instance, the family had changed sides! Easily his most successful work was his *Life of George Eliot*. Published in 1887, and written with warmth and personal knowledge, it sold well right from the start, and remains in print, even today, in a reissue of 1972. Like all his books, it was full of mistakes – what he forgot he just invented. But, as an intimate recollection of someone whose life he had really admired, written with characteristic style – crisp, simple, and straight to the point – almost like a private letter, it brought her complex character to life and carried a stamp of authenticity.

He gave a copy to Benjamin Jowett, the awesome Master of Balliol College, who said in acknowledgement, 'I write to thank you for sending me the life of George Eliot which I have read with great interest. I think that any friend of hers will be glad that you wrote it. It appears to me to put her character in a very true light as far as I knew her.' O.B. must have been pleased with this, for praise from Jowett was hard to win, and any praise from him was praise indeed.[1]

O.B.'s histories also earned him a large and popular following. A firm adherent to the Seeley school which believed that history's ebb and flow was governed by laws ordained by God, and that such laws could be ascertained and used in a scientific manner, his work was always direct and plain, and described simple causes and effects which appeared to illustrate natural laws. Thus in tune with orthodox opinion, he appealed widely to a diverse public.

In particular his essay, *The Flight to Varennes*, a vivid account of the fatal attempt by the doomed Louis XVI and Marie Antoinette to reach the safety of the eastern frontier of France, gained him a wide and admiring readership. He explored the route to Varennes himself, puffing over the dusty road which he joined at Chalons, south of Reims, on his new hayfork 'Meteor' tricycle. It had two large wheels in front, fitted with the latest solid tyres, a padded seat instead of a saddle, and was steered by the right hand with a lever which was linked to a smaller wheel at the back. He described the journey in lively style, ranging variously over the theme, considering the weather, the state of the roads, the size of the carriages, the position of the inns, and many other factual details; also the critical human errors which led the plan, so near success, to end in total disaster. The result was a really telling account which still remains of genuine interest today.

His heavier works were another matter. His *Peter the Great, Charles XII*, volumes of diplomatic despatches and his studies of mediaeval Europe were little more than historical pap, although they sold in large numbers and in some cases in several editions. Men like his former colleague, Prothero, the professor of modern history at Edinburgh, felt affronted that popular success should be built on such a light foundation – on tricycle trips to battlefields and cities, and on mere charm and readability. Whenever they could, they said so plainly. A critic in the *Guardian* spoke for them all when he wrote in August 1895,

The Age of the Condottieri by Oscar Browning, Author of *Guelphs and Ghibellines* (Methuen). Mr. Oscar Browning has published another volume of his funny little history of Italy in the middle ages. It is as naive and characteristically slipshod as the previous volume. He calls it *The Age of the Condottieri*, but that, in 'Alice in Wonderland' fashion, is what it is called and not what it is. There is very little about the Condottieri in it at all, and certainly no attempt to estimate their influence as an institution upon Italy . . . Nevertheless, if the reader is not particular about grammar and style, and is judiciously suspicious of dates, he, or more likely she, will derive both amusement and profit from Mr. Browning's pages.

Such criticism naturally hurt, and O.B. wrote and complained to the editor, who only made things worse by repeating the critic's actual words, that the book was both 'grotesque and slipshod'.

All the same, like it or not, this was the truth and O.B. knew it. It was true, too, of other works, and he actually said of one

The man of the day

production, his *New Illustrated History of England*, that he wrote it only for 'grocers and cheesemongers'. This remark reached his publishers who naturally enough asked him to deny it: he did so at once without a qualm. But it was so typical of the tart condescension with which he normally treated such people and so aptly described this illustrated hotchpotch of a book that no denial was of any use. All who knew him remained convinced he had said it.

The book itself was in four volumes, each of 100,000 words, for which he received £300, a fair sum, at least for him, as much as the annual income of his Fellowship. In many ways, he scarcely earned it. He was always slow in submitting the copy, and was so late with one instalment that he was never even sent a proof. So it contained mistakes as usual. One reader, protesting from Edinburgh, called it an 'educational absurdity'.

In spite of criticism, O.B. worked extremely hard and was justly praised by his friends for his industry. A chance encounter with A.J. Balfour, the elder brother of his friend, Gerald, who was then First Lord of the Treasury, produced the following letter of which O.B. must have been proud.[2]

4, Carlton Gardens, S.W.
2nd April 1891

My dear Browning
    I most sincerely trust you do not think that the observation I hazarded on the steps of the Athenaeum was intended as a criticism. I think the list of works which you sent me put to shame many persons who consider themselves very industrious. I at least should consider that I have reached heights of energy never hitherto attained if I could look back upon such a catalogue of performances.
    I know how broken up University life is, and I attribute it in part to the abominable system of managing everything through syndicates or committees – ingenious contrivances for making the work of ten wise men as if it were inferior to the work of one fool.
    Thanks much for your article on Greek. I have read it with great interest and considerable agreement though I have my doubts

whether history ought to take quite as high rank educationally as you give it.

Yours very Sincerely, Arthur James Balfour

In January 1895, a long expected event occurred which for a moment gave O.B. a chance of official recognition. This was the death of Sir John Seeley, the Regius Professor of History at Cambridge. Almost before the body was cold, O.B. wrote to Lord Rosebery, the Prime Minister, to ask to be given the appointment. Like many other statesmen of the day, Rosebery knew O.B. from his time at Eton; knew him too as a Liberal candidate, being the Liberal leader himself; and knew him again, like everyone else, as a leading Cambridge eccentric. Unhappily, also, he knew quite well that O.B.'s claims to scholarship were slight, and that all the popular books in the world were not sufficient to make him a professor. He advised the Queen to appoint Lord Acton, a wise choice in every respect, and one that O.B. could not condemn, being himself Lord Acton's admirer.

O.B. felt bitter for a long time, casting the blame on the jealousy of others, ambitious colleagues, unknown enemies, who must have advised Lord Rosebery against him. In this, for once, he was perfectly correct, although the motive was not jealousy. The undergraduates had thought it a lark and had taken the matter with mock seriousness. 'T'O.B. or not t'O.B . . .' they had joked. The dons had not been amused at all. Near panic had gripped the Establishment at the thought of O.B. succeeding Seeley, and, as the Rosebery archives show, strenuous efforts were made to prevent it.[3]

The outcome only convinced O.B. that his fame outside the academic world had created deep resentment within it. At Eton, at King's, and now at the University itself, his pre-eminent claim failed to achieve the notice it deserved. For a while he felt depressed and defeated, although when Lord Acton's name was announced he welcomed him at once with sincere generosity, and even wrote to Lord Rosebery again to say how much he applauded the appointment. Then, a new excitement occurred. He was asked to contest a seat for the Liberals in a general election called in the spring. Once again his morale revived as he drafted speeches and met supporters. His chance of winning a seat was slight but all past failures were forgotten in the proud and demanding public struggle to become a Member of Parliament.

O.B.'s political career, if such it may be called, in fact consisted of three contests: Norwood in 1886, Worcestershire in 1892, Derbyshire in 1895. The second provides the best account of his platform manner, views and behaviour. This was the one he most enjoyed, the one which, in his own opinion, justly established his reputation as a truly committed Liberal supporter.

This election was won by the Liberals, the last under the leadership of 'The Grand Old Man'. The principal issue was whether or not Home Rule should be granted to an Irish Government. Six years earlier the party had split on this same intractable issue, and had lost the resulting general election. The breakaway faction, the Liberal Unionists – those whose views remained Liberal except on the question of the Irish Union – had joined forces with the Conservatives. At that time in East Worcestershire (the seat O.B. was about to contest) the Liberal member had become a Unionist, from the Liberal point of view betraying those who had given him his place. Thus, in the coming general election, the Gladstone party with O.B. had a real opportunity at long last to win back the seat and take revenge. Against him, however, was a young opponent who had not only local claims but also a special political advantage. He was none other than Austen Chamberlain, son of Joseph Chamberlain, the former Mayor of Birmingham and leader of the Unionist party in the Commons. Still, it was thought before the poll that the middle-aged don and the youthful student – O.B. was fifty-five and his boyish adversary twenty-nine – had each an even chance of winning the contest.

As both men knew each other well – Chamberlain had been at Trinity, Cambridge, and a member of O.B.'s Political Society – and as they both respected and liked each other, they decided independently to fight the contest on politics alone, and avoid personal invective entirely.

Of course, within this friendly limit they allowed themselves a certain licence. Chamberlain quoted an Irish newspaper, the *Dublin Daily Independent*, which called O.B. a 'political huckster' who peddled a useless patent medicine, in other words, Home Rule. O.B. retorted with the help of Shakespeare. 'The Dream' was having a local performance, and the press reported that Chamberlain had watched it. O.B. made his audience laugh in a speech at Dodford shortly afterwards, saying his opponent was like Titania, bewitched and in love with a bottomless ass, in other words, with Conservative policy.

Here, in the hamlets surrounding Bromsgrove, he and his promises went down well. One man, one vote, the introduction of Parish Councils; these and other Liberal proposals for the better condition of the working classes, especially those who depended on agriculture, were all things that he really believed in. He spoke informally, as in a classroom, without flourish or bombast. If the working people alone had voted – those of Redditch, Catshill and Sidemoor, even those of King's Heath, the Chamberlain family's own parish – O.B. would likely have been successful. As it was, there were also townsmen, prosperous clerks and opulent businessmen, who lived locally but worked in Birmingham, who to a man were Liberal Unionists. Also the Chamberlain family name drew towards it many waverers. In a poll of nearly eight thousand, Chamberlain won by two to one. The High Sheriff announced the result from the old Town Hall of Bromsgrove on the 9th July at half-past two. Austen Chamberlain's supporters cheered and so, too, did O.B., shaking Chamberlain's hand delightedly.

O.B. had achieved a result he desired, the fulfilment of one of his main ambitions. He had gained practical experience with which to improve his lectures on history and politics, for the preparation of men like Chamberlain for the highest tasks of arduous statesmanship. The night before the votes had been counted he had lain awake, pondering the issue, wondering what he really wanted – a don's life or a politician's, two worlds so very different, so very hard to combine successfully. Now that the issue was finally settled, he was quite content to accept the result. Without doubt his defeat was a blessing. He would never have been a success in the Commons. He was far too difficult and uncompromising, his love of what he called debate being nothing more than self assertion, unbridled vanity, and an obsessive and ever expanding desire for continual personal advertisement.

In this respect he had scored a triumph. Five thousand copies of his photograph –an 'Election Special' by the *Bromsgrove Messenger* – showing him kindly, wise and pure ('a beautiful face', as someone said) had been carried abroad by squads of bicyclists. A group of ardent Liberal enthusiasts had even founded a club in his honour, the Oscar Browning Club of Worcestershire.

On the national front he had scored, too, thanks to having as an opponent the son of the leading Liberal Unionist. Had he fought an ordinary person his name might never have reached the limelight. As it was, opposing a Chamberlain, it appeared in all the major newspapers, not only throughout the United Kingdom but also in all the election reports that reached the farthest corners of the Empire. On a personal level he had scored also, making new, amusing friends, not least amongst the young, who had written him many delightful letters. Howard Hinton, a local schoolboy, addressed him proudly after the election,[4]

> Dear Mr. Browning. I am now having the pleasure of writing to one I wish could have been a member of Parliament if all the people of East Worcestershire had been sensible. I had your letter, and after showing it all round at school carefully placed it in my drawer with your card for safety, the Unionists tried in vain to get it off me for there are out of 21 boys
> 9 Gladstonians
> 3 Liberal Unionists
> 9 Conservative Unionists
> and it is the best class in the school for the other classes are mostly 2/3 Unionists, and a few 5/6 Unionists. We have political meetings

at school and in the train and my Gladstonian friend Crofts helps me and we find the Unionists can only make fun of Gladstone and you and all the rest of the Gladstonians, but we soon put them down and ask them to prove anything wrong in Home Rule *but they* can't nor could anyone else with sense . . . Those silk worms of mine have begun to spin it is curious to watch them spinning almost as curious as to watch them eat. All those young pigeons have grown up and are sold.

Remaining Your loving friend (and true follower)
Howard Hinton

His own 'Oscar Browning Club', whick kept his name before the world, also generated correspondence. Of its formation, his agent had told him, 'One kind friend suggests the perpetuation of your association with East Worcestershire by the formation of an "Oscar Browning Club" on the model of the Eighty Club to undertake missionary work in the Division – to such heights of political enthusiasm have you raised one who is not either "young & foolish" or "old & childish".'[5]

Who this supporter was is not recorded in the Browning Archive. Perhaps he wished to remain anonymous. Whoever he was, he rallied his friends and put his proposal into effect, specially printing Club notepaper which bore O.B.'s election portrait. For many months letters arrived telling O.B. of the Club's activities. These gave him infinite pleasure. He showed them to all his friends at Cambridge until, at length, they begged him to desist. He belonged to a club called The Epicureans, an undergraduate debating society at which, whatever was being discussed, he spoke of himself and his recent campaign. Finally, everyone began to remonstrate, and the Secretary recorded that after this he did speak for ten minutes 'without alluding to East Worcestershire'.

Finally, he had scored a triumph, too, amongst the students who did not know him by being solemnly teased in *The Granta*. It proposed a Modern Literature Tripos in which a question read as follows:[6]

4 (a) 'Mr. Oscar Browning is not so much one don as an epitome of all Cambridge.'

The man of the day

Discuss this statement and give a list of all the clubs with which Mr. Browning is, or has been connected.
(b) State your opinion of the theory which attributes to his authorship the poems circulating under the name of 'Robert Browning.'
(c) Where is East Worcestershire? Illustrate your answer by a map showing the situation of the parties, the position of Mr. Browning, the attitude of Mr. Chamberlain and the aspect of affairs.

[(a) must be attempted, and *either* (b) *or* (c) but *not both*]

To discuss the statement in section (a) would, in fact, have been very easy. The short answer was simply 'Yes'. O.B. *was* the epitome of Cambridge; and everyone who read the pages of *The Granta* soon realised that this was the case. From the point of view of the undergraduates no don in the university began to approach him in prodigality. Everything he said was handed round, and everything he did was the subject of a joke. From the very first issue of *The Granta*, in the Lent term of 1889, he had been depicted by successive editors as 'The glory, jest, and riddle of the World'. In the 270 numbers which stretched over ten years only one had gone to press without printing his name at all; without even a jocular reference to the many student clubs and societies of which he was either president or chairman. This was produced as a special issue which in itself was a major tribute.[7] It was, as the editor wrote, 'AN EXPERIMENT. In order to watch the effect upon our circulation, and to test to the full the self-denial of our readers, we propose to issue, next week, as an entirely original, unheard of, and almost incredible departure, a whole number of *The Granta* containing absolutely no mention whatever of Mr. Oscar Browning.'

The joke was enjoyed, and O.B. loved it. The issue which followed, brought him back. Commenting on the end of a term in which nothing had changed and nothing had happened the editor said, with customary banter, '*Omnia Mutantur* yes, but in Cambridge we are unchanged, the same sameness has pervaded everything – our Dons, our undergraduates, our tradesmen, our "touts", our beef in hall, and the cut of our waistcoats.

112

The man of the day

The drains and the Fellow of King's, who we may not mention but whom we leave to your imagination, we have ever with us.' This was the last issue of the term; indeed, the very last of the nineteenth century.

The secret of O.B.'s popular appeal lay as much as anything else in his quite extraordinary appearance. Once of perfectly normal proportions, never tall but reasonably slim, in middle age he began to shrink and slowly and steadily become inflated. The famous epigram about his bulk, composed in 1886, shortly before his fiftieth birthday, was not the first of many warnings that he ought to pay attention to his figure. For a short while he took it to heart, consulting a Mr J.F. Little, a man who had suffered from overweight himself and who had been relieved by the following diet:[8]

> DAILY: to drink five pints of water or weak tea with lemon at 130 degrees fahrenheit; a pound of cold beefsteak ($1\frac{1}{4}$ inches thick and not overdone) at 8.30 a.m. A pound and a quarter at 1.30 p.m. and a pound at 6.30 p.m. *No fluid with the solids*. The beef to be varied with undercut of sirloin, hare, pheasant, blackcock, etc., hot or cold. To be eaten slowly and masticated thoroughly. Mr. Gladstone's thirty-two 'chews' are about right.

Perhaps remembering indigestion, even possibly an attack of lock-jaw when he himself had eaten thus, Little ended up with some simpler advice, 'a stewed apple or a few stewed prunes to help the food down and relieve the bowels'.

As O.B.'s girth steadily increased, it is more than likely that Little's advice was read and then enjoyably ignored. Since he always wolfed his meals, partly out of simple greed, for he loved food of every description, and partly because he wanted to talk – in middle-age he did so incessantly – he would have found the 'chews' alone a penance.

To watch him eat also was a penance. Arthur Benson, his former pupil, who like O.B. had returned to Cambridge after a spell as an Eton housemaster, was spellbound with disgust by the way O.B. behaved at table.

'Dined in Hall', Benson wrote in his diary.[9] 'O.B. again

113

talking literature at me with gross compliments, holding morsels in his lips, like a parrot or some seed-eating bird . . .' 'Again . . . he rolled about; he ate and drank, he made horrible noises, held his red silk handkerchief *in his mouth*! He has a horrible habit of eating & talking with his mouth open, like a parrot eating seeds. As he speaks, long strings of meat, fragments of bread, come to the front of his mouth & appear on his teeth like calves scampering to look over a hedge; & are then horribly withdrawn. I looked at him with disgust.'[10]

In November 1888, O.B. was paid the supreme and ultimate honour of being cartooned in *Vanity Fair*, the first Cambridge don to appear in the nineteen years of its weekly appearance. He was rather nervous before it came out, and begged the artist to treat him kindly. 'I am amused at your want of belief in me,' W.B. Hayes assured him. 'Could I make anyone supremely ridiculous? I assure you that in your case I have no desire beyond a strongly characteristic likeness.'

In fact he failed, and no one liked it. O.B.'s family thought it 'cruel', and his friends agreed it had 'no resemblance'. However, this had no importance. Its publication was the thing that mattered, and what was written by 'Jehu' beside it. Only seven other dons had ever been given similar publicity. All these had been at Oxford: Benjamin Jowett, Edward Pusey, the Warden of Merton, the Dean of Pembroke, and three prominent, learned professors.

O.B. was simply delighted. No one could possibly assert now that outside Cambridge nobody knew him or that within it his fame was illusory. His colleagues bit their lips with annoyance, a fact that delighted him even more. 'Of course there will be jealousy & all that', Hayes wrote when O.B. told him about it, 'but so there would be about the Archangel Gabriel'.[11] Whether or not it was a good likeness, everyone wanted to buy a copy. Three hundred extra prints had to be sent express to Cambridge. O.B. ordered them by the dozen; and with a shy and genial smile, gave them to all his colleagues, friends and acquaintances.

As to the text which ran beside it, he liked this almost even more. 'The first founder of King's College, Cambridge, was Henry VI; the second was Mr. Oscar Browning.' What, he asked, could be truer than that? 'By authority of the Queen in Council, there are forty-six Fellows of the College – by unanimous agreement of the men of Cambridge, there is one . . . He is the life and soul of the Society which has the good fortune to possess him, and his schemes for the benefaction of mankind are as capacious as the tails of his coat . . . he is a good Fellow of whom Cambridge is deservedly proud.' Thus 'Jehu Junior' described him. Anyone taking *The Granta* 'Tripos' which was set so gaily four years later had only to echo *Vanity Fair* to obtain an honours pass with flying colours.

Apart from O.B.'s extraordinary shape – his short legs, balloon-like stomach, and round head, completely bald except for a fringe of curls at the neck – which made him such a figure of fun and assured his place as a popular eccentric, his renown amongst the undergraduates came from his friendly personality. Not only was he agreeable to all, and proved his embracing love of youth by his open gatherings on Sunday evenings, but also he showed his desire to help in many different ways by his membership of all their clubs and societies.

He was President, Treasurer, Chairman or Secretary of more than a dozen organisations and hardly a student club existed, whether for sport or psychical research, for music, drama or social converse, of which he was not at least a patron.

In spite of his many regular commitments – his public lectures, private tutorials, his Political Society, his Liberal Club, his Dante group, his Sunday 'at homes' – he found time to support them all. He was also Treasurer of the Union Society, a post he held for twenty-one years. He always, somehow, managed to appear, always late, always smiling, and always saying 'How awfully jolly!' The undergraduates loved him for it. His amiable manner, positive attitude, his ever-readiness to make a speech, sing a song or take part in a game, made him a welcome figure at every gathering.

Everything he did was reported in *The Granta*. As the editor told him on one occasion, 'You energise so variously and so constantly in Cambridge that our W.P.B. overflows with contributions – praise, chaff, *que sais-je* – written about you.'[12]

The Footlights gave an admirable smoker on Saturday, at which Messrs Knapp and Anderson were especially good. The President [O.B.] also obliged with 'The Baby on the Shore', and 'The Little-Go'. There is a particular pathos about the line 'We sat upon the baby on the shore' when it is sung by the President of the Footlights. The remarkable part of it is that the baby is ever heard of again.[13]

The treasurer (of the Union) was delightful. His humour was as broad as his genial smile. His election experiences were 'all told', and by several of his accounts he is fond of Turkish baths. He has been chatting with Mr. Gladstone 'who may be considered a competent authority'. Really, what *should* we do without the treasurer on big nights?[14]

The familiar form of Mr. Oscar Browning has been missed of late at the bathing sheds. The yokels of Granchester are complaining that they cannot now see the evergreen Don sitting on the highest elevation swathed in a towel and smoking a cigarette. Mr. Browning used to serve as a landmark for pedestrians near Cambridge when King's Chapel and the new Roman Catholic Church were invisible.[15]

> From Timbuctoo to distant Downing
> Who has not heard of Osc*r Br*wn*ng?
>
> In shape he is something like a roller;
> He wears a most impressive bowler.
>
> He'll give you a lot of useful tips
> On emperors, and ghosts, and gyps
>
> Abroad he's very widely known;
> His smile would melt a pumice stone.[16]

Also, in almost every issue there was either a joke or an illustration (the same applied in the many other student ephemera). Whatever the burning local issue, whatever the grave national dilemma, from the Union decision to build a laundry to the controversial Boer War, there was soon to be found an absurd tale which somehow included 'Caro Oscaro', or else a portrait or caricature. Whether described as O.B.[2] in some long, involved, insoluble equation, or shown pedalling away to Africa, half clown, half soldier, leaving King's on his famous tricycle, he was once more offered to the public as something Cambridge often stood for: a mixture of fun and serious concern for the world beyond its comfortable colleges.

Finally, in almost every number of *The Granta* he was teased for his monumental snobbery. In this field he was not alone, his chief rival being Dr Waldstein, archaeologist and Slade Professor, who often managed to trump him at Cambridge by catching the best visiting notables and showing them round the Fitzwilliam museum. However, when it came to the holidays O.B. outplayed the Professor easily. Wherever he went he 'signed the book' of all the Emperors, Kings or Princes in whose domains he happened to be; and having a respected name in Europe as a leading English educationalist (much more so than he had at Cambridge) he often captured an invitation. 'The nicest Emperor I ever met', became a famous O.B. catchword, spoken about the Emperor of Austria whom he – O.B. – greeted at Maloja near St Moritz draped in a flowing Roman toga, accompanied by four undergraduates, bearing wands and dressed as lictors.

Once he had met them, he sent them his books: his *Guelphs and Ghibellines* to Queen Victoria; his *Peter the Great* to the Emperor of Russia; his *Charles XII* to the King of Sweden; his own photograph to the Queen of Spain which, her Lady in Waiting informed him, 'Her Majesty graciously deigns to accept'. One letter from the Duke of Edinburgh, the fourth child of Queen Victoria, to whom he sent a copy of his *Goethe* must have given him extra pleasure. Having thanked him with customary charm the Duke concluded with royal innocence that he always retained a pleasant remembrance of the two times they had bathed together at the St George's baths.

His greatest coup, which never came off, was making friends

with the Duke of Clarence who came to Cambridge in 1883. The Duke was the Prince of Wales's son, and therefore heir to the throne itself. O.B. tried to get him for King's, but in the end he went to Trinity. O.B. got to know him, however, through a former pupil, J.K. Stephen, who had been appointed the Duke's tutor. It was almost more than O.B. could bear to be so near and yet so far from fulfilling his avowed life's ambition of guiding the mind of a youthful prince, especially a reigning monarch's grandson who would one day rule an empire. He saw him on every available occasion, and as soon as possible entertained him. He invited him, first, to various meals, was received back for repasts in return, and towards Christmas a year later felt on sufficiently intimate terms to give himself the infinite delight of sending the Duke a 'little cigarette case'. He even took to playing hockey, a game at which he was perfectly hopeless but of which the Duke was extremely fond, for the sole purpose of being near him and receiving a princely whack on the shins. Unhappily, everything came to nothing. The Duke died, eight years later, and all O.B. was able to do was to write a long obituary in *The Granta*.[17]

His love of the great as reported in *The Granta* was an endless source of amusement to all, not the least to O.B. himself who delighted in every kind of publicity. His snobbery somehow stirred an emotion that was latent in the hearts of many of the young, and the more he boasted about the monarchs to whom he had bowed during the vacation or from whom he had just received a letter, the more he was begged to keep it up and maintain his lead over Dr Waldstein.

'Mr Browning must look to his laurels. I saw Dr Waldstein sitting next to a prince of the blood at the last night of the A.D.C. The score now is "game ball all" with Dr Waldstein leading by a prince and an emperor in the "set 3".'[18] 'In the course of conversation with Mr Oscar Browning, of King's, I asked him how Dr Waldstein was getting on in Greece. The reply was characteristic: "Well, my dear fellow, I hope that he is behaving himself, and I hope still more that my poor friend King George is not taking his advice. Ha! ha! ha!" '[19]

8 OB with Day Training College students, 1900

9 'Mid-Term Tea at Mr Oscar Browning's', 1908. Max Beerbohm's cartoon of OB, undergraduates and assorted crowned heads of Europe

10 OB by Ignazio Zuloaga, 1900

The man of the day

THE ROYAL VISIT TO CAMBRIDGE. *The Granta*, of course, sent a reporter to make notes of the reception of the Duchess of York in Cambridge on Thursday, by Mr. Oscar Browning. There seems to have been a procession of Judges and a Circus in Cambridge on the same day, and what with the dazzling splendour of Royalty, the magnificence of Mr. Oscar Browning and, it may be, the pleasurable effects of lunch, my note-taker appears to have mixed up the Royal Party with the Imperial Lord George Sanger's Circus, and the ermined dispensers of justice. However, I print his notes as I received them, and leave him to explain matters to the Duchess and to Mr. Oscar Browning.

'It was a windy morning', writes *The Granta* reporter, 'and the awe produced by impending royalty, the respect which every Cambridge man owes to the majestic presence of Mr. Oscar Browning, and the raw state of the atmosphere combined I must confess to produce a slight trembling in the limbs. Punctually to the moment the train steamed into the station amidst the enthusiastic applause of the loyal townspeople of Cambridge. The Duchess looked charming in a dress of' – (I omit two pages evidently intended for the *Gentlewoman.*) 'She was immediately conducted with her retinue to the gilded car drawn by the celebrated team of piebald performing horses. Mr. Oscar Browning then mounted "Alonzo", the largest African Elephant in the world, and waved the Field Marshal's baton, presented to him by H.I.M. the German Emperor, as a signal for the procession to start.'[20]

O.B.'s friendship with the Teck family represented his finest achievement. The young duchess became Queen Mary; and up to the very end of his life he managed, proudly, to keep in tenuous touch with her.

Thus, as he moved into middle-age, in spite of the snubs and rebuffs of his colleagues – for in King's itself he remained isolated – he looked round at his obvious successes, his literary output and his popularity; and he still believed that the day would come when his work and achievements would be appreciated. After all, his reputation as a patron of youth and educationalist, successful author and friend of princes, had not been gained by doing nothing. Even in 1884, well before his personality had made him one of the lions of Cambridge, his reputation as a leading teacher had grown beyond the academic sphere. As a result he had been cartooned with other celebrities in a weekly journal almost as famous as *Vanity Fair*.

In a special Christmas number of *The World*, in a comic survey of the year's events, a reporter had written from the Mountains of the Moon of a week spent with 'Dr Mahdi' discussing the making of a constitution – an allusion to the infant Belgian Congo – to whom, of course, he had to say in the ever popular manner of Stanley, 'Dr Mahdi, I presume?' After the text, on two pages, all the prominent men of the day had been drawn as explorers marching to Africa, half naked and carrying weapons, to give their advice to the spiritual leader. In a crocodile queue with a hundred others – Dean Farrar, the Duke of Argyll, Tennyson, Ruskin, Manning, Millais, Lord Salisbury, Mr Gladstone – O.B. had been included.

He had been depicted next but one to a figure holding a spear which transfixed a lily: none other than Oscar Wilde. The juxtaposition here was significant. Eleven years were still to pass before Wilde went to prison, and before the innocent man in the street saw the aesthetes as homosexuals. After Wilde's shattering disaster, many people suddenly remembered how often he and O.B. had met, how often their names had appeared together; and they saw truly, how once again, coming events had cast their shadows before them.

CHAPTER X

Family affairs, and Robbie Ross

In the summer of 1889, the year after *Vanity Fair* had published O.B.'s caricature and crowned him prince of the dons at Cambridge, his mother died. O.B., against his will, found he had to take her place as head of the Browning family.

Already in 1886, events had made him play this role in the case of the family distillery. It had been in decline for many years, and when his brother, Arthur, had died – he had moved it down from London to Lewes but failed to keep it a going concern – it had quietly gone into liquidation. Not quietly enough, however, for the final blow had come from Frederick, Arthur's son, who had run away with the last of the money. He had been arrested and sent to prison. On release, with O.B.'s help and that of kind friends in Lewes who had clubbed together and raised some funds, he had been discreetly hidden away and later spirited off to western America.

O.B.'s part in this disaster had been as his brother's executor. Under the terms of the latter's will, he had been obliged to continue the business, to pay Frederick £100 per year to deal with the ordinary daily affairs, and, of course, to account for the profits. At first it had sounded simple enough. He had seen Frederick from time to time and been told that the business was doing well. He had signed leases and other documents; and knowing nothing of deficit finance like loans, mortgages and notes of hand, he had left these things to the family solicitor.

Then, suddenly, Frederick had vanished, and all the troubles in the legal world had fallen directly on O.B.'s shoulders. He had found himself personally liable for all the profits he had not received, and even after going to court and getting a formal absolution with a payment of three shillings in the pound, he had never convinced his brother's family that all the fault had not been his but that of their own professional advisers.

Family affairs, and Robbie Ross

Now, in 1889, still in the aftermath of the storm with many matters yet unsettled, his mother's death left him alone. Throughout these very difficult years in this and a dozen other matters, indeed in every domestic problem, he had always turned to her for advice. For the very first time in his life, at the sober age of fifty-two, he found himself at last without a comforter.

Mrs Browning's letters to her son reveal the tender bond of their relationship.[1]

The Beehive
Osborne Road
Windsor

July 6th 1885

Thank you, my dear Oscar, for your scraps telling me your movements, etc. I like to think I know where you are. Harrow speech day was a grand affair, putting Eton into the shade. I am glad you did not speak to the Provost & Mrs Hornby, that you had never condescended to shake hands with them – I could not have done it – Mrs Provost gave a garden party on Saturday. It was said that Princess Christina and Mrs Gladstone were to be there. At any rate they did not make an appearance, and I hear that the whole affair was *very dull*. Why is it, my dear Boy, that you have never been in the first rank like Welldon, Selwyn & so on. Surely your fame will live after you, for how much have you not contributed to the making (of) these men. I have so much ambition for you . . . God bless you, my dear Boy. When are you coming to look at the old lady again.

Yr loving & devoted Mother, Mariana

All her letters contained sentiments in much the same affectionate strain, showing her love as well as distress that her darling boy had not succeeded, had not the rewards she knew he deserved. He was clever, popular, and known to everyone. Yet he remained a simple don without even the title of Professor. She felt an increasing sense of anxiety as the years passed and nothing happened, as no *magnum opus* appeared, as no important post was secured, and as she herself, in her middle eighties, began to suffer the frailties of age.

... When will you run down to see your old mother? ... God bless you my dear child – don't bother about trifles, dont be *old maidish* ...

... Your welcome letter has just arrived, it cheers me to know that you are well & happy – tho' I grieve for the obesity. Why drink beer, why not seltzer water? ...

... Tell me my dear Boy what you are about & when I shall have a chance of seeing your dear face again. I rejoyce that you are well. Are you thinner – your sister Mina is treading in your steps – uncommonly stout. God bless you, my very dear Oscar.

Your letter last evening caused me a sleepless night – do let me hear how you are. You must have taken cold on that horrible crossing, and now the damp of our atmosphere, everywhere redolent of falling leaves, and I was congratulating myself on your looking so well, and *not so fat* ... write but a line to assure your anxious Mother.

Thanks for your always expected and always welcome letter. That you are full of works I doubt not, but I am sorry that your cold is still not better. This capricious climate is ill suited to *our* delicate frames. I have had a cold and am now suffering from neuralgia which is most tiresome & depressing ... Let me hear soon, your letters are an Elixir vitae to me. God bless & keep you my dear Boy prays ever yr affec Mother.

I rather forestalled my answer to your usual weekly communication by writing on Saturday. I suppose my letter reached you altho' you do not notice any of its contents ... I wish the government would create a 'Minister of Education' and give the appointment to you. That is my ambition, not to see you one of a herd of political Radicals clammering for they know not what and making bad worse ... The undergraduate at Trinity that I want you to notice is Bowring, one of 14 sons and one sister who is here and a charming girl. The boy was at Eton, I forget in whose house ...

The last letter in Mrs Browning's file, in a very wobbly hand, reads:

Family affairs, and Robbie Ross

The Beehive
Osborne Road
Windsor

St. Patrick's Day

My darling. Will the art of G. Eliot interest the boys – is it not over their heads! My heart is set on your success, my ambition.

God bless you Better but weak Mariana

O.B.'s utter sense of loss when the weekly letters came to an end, when he had to grapple with family decisions without his mother's advice and support; when no one cared whether he was fat, or climbed the ladder of worldly success, was something from which he never really recovered.

Like many people who are bereaved he felt that the loved-one's vibrant spirit could not, simply, have disappeared. Being a member of the Society for Psychical Research which used to meet in his rooms at King's he consulted a medium, Mrs Piper, who tried to reach his mother in a trance. The result was not very satisfactory. Mrs Piper closed her eyes and told O.B. that he smoked too much. However, she gave a 'strong impression' that Mrs Browning's spirit hovered near.

More tangible consolation came from O.B.'s friends and colleagues. Letters arrived at King's in shoals, the greatest number from Old Etonians, boys who had been in O.B.'s house who had known Mrs Browning personally. One and all comprehended as only the pure in heart could, in those days before analysis had probed the mother-and-son relationship, how deep a shock her death would be.

In a note sent by Dr Waldstein, O.B.'s colleague and arch rival in the joyful game of catching royalties, all their feelings were fully expressed.[2]

King's College
Cambridge
June 13th 1889

My Dear Browning,

I have just this moment heard of the sad loss that has befallen you and I hasten to express to you the deep sympathy which I – & I

124

am certain many others here – feel with you.

I am sure that the wider one's interests & sympathies, the greater the corresponding need of a centralised affection. You & I have found this in our mothers. You must have realised with me, that, however kind one's friends & however warm one's feelings for them the lasting, unchanging & long suffering love of a mother excels – profoundly strong in its simple tender & homely features. I know this well, and I weep with you.

Yours fraternally Chas Waldstein

The person who felt the loss, however, in its most immediate and painful form was O.B.'s sister, Mariana. Known as 'Dick' within the family, perhaps to avoid confusion with her mother, she had spent the previous fourteen years running a small school for girls. At the same time she had cared for her mother. 'The blank to me is inexpressible', she wrote to O.B. after the funeral. Now in her forty-seventh year, she had never left home in her life except for a week or two in the holidays. She it was who endured the sorrow of going back to an empty house, of tidying up a silent room, of moving aside a vacant chair, and all the other poignant tasks of a recent family bereavement.

However, at least she had the school. She and her mother had moved to Windsor after the Eton house had closed. It belonged to the College and had to be surrendered. Since O.B. had ceased to support them, and because neither had any money, she had opened up a girls' school which became known as The Beehive.

'Miss Browning, living with her mother, receives into her home. a limited number of pupils.' Thus had read the first advertisement. Eight girls had come at the start, sisters of boys who were still at Eton. They wore 'hard, hideous, sailor hats, terribly stiff, high collars', and frocks with buttons down the back. They lodged in two adjoining houses at 1 Queen's Gardens, Osborne Road.

Mariana was a perfect example of the way in which, in Victorian times, a well-educated single woman could find herself fighting against tremendous odds to survive and keep up appearances. Nearly all the three hundred surviving letters she wrote to O.B. mention problems connected with money. So long as she kept her school full, the maximum number was twenty-six, she was able to live in a state of gentility. The moment, however, the numbers fell – in one terrible summer term a girl died and others went home – she found herself on the brink of absolute poverty.

Then she had to write for help, and not always in the gentlest terms. If O.B. was generous to some – his little friends and his favourite pupils – he was not so to Mariana. He preferred to give her brotherly advice, and quite naturally from time to time she sent it back with compound interest.

> My dear Oscar [she once wrote], You speak of yourself as my natural helper & protector; I think if you calmly & dispassionately look back to the time when I began my work here, you will see that neither by advice or in any other way have you helped me. Twice I have asked for your advice, once in 1884 when I was in great money difficulty, once since, & both times your answer was such as to make me feel it was useless to ask again. Remissively since I began my work, you have given me *absolutely* no help, on the contrary, for several years of my mother's life, you omitted the allowance you had promised her, thus throwing the whole burden upon me, which she felt keenly, more so than you have any idea of.[3]

Another time she told him, 'I know you will be surprised to hear that I am leaving Windsor after Xmas & moving my school to Bexhill. Ever since I had diptheria my school has gone down, my receipts dropped £1000 in 6 months, & I am losing now at least £500 a year . . . Now I want to know if you will lend me £200 or £300 for my move etc. I have a very little money invested which I do not want to draw out as it is making money & gives me very good interest.' After the move she asked again:

> I always feel that you do not really take an interest in my work, especially when it is a work of struggle as mine is now. If I can tide over the next 6 months I hope to get on here as I have many applications, but I need about £200 or £300 to carry me through & I know that this is not pleasant for you to hear, of course I never

can forget that my brother never gave me any help towards my work, & that not only that but that I really paid you £600 in money after my mother died. I fear I shall never have the money Biscoe owes me, & those of my family whom I have helped & educated, have I fear, done harm to the Beehive & certainly are not inclined to help me now. Bexhill is a very uninteresting place but the air is splendid & my girls love it.

At last O.B. agreed to help, and from this time onwards matters improved. The school became a great success, and was not again in financial straits until the beginning of the 1960s. Then, at length, in other circumstances, in a new era with different needs, it moved at first to larger premises and finally closed down.

The person to whom Mariana referred, to whom she had generously lent money, from whom she never expected payment, was her elder sister's husband, Biscoe Wortham. If Mariana had financial worries, her sister's problems were infinitely worse. Like Mariana, in a different way, she too was a perfect example of a widely acknowledged Victorian type. She had married a feckless, bankrupt clergyman and had absolutely no money. Her fight to maintain their social standing in a highly stratified, critical world, with attendant sickness and humiliation was more courageous, painful and dramatic than anything found in the cheapest yellow novel.

This sister who was known as Mina (a shortened form of her name, Malvina) had married Biscoe in 1870 in the happy days when the family were still at Eton. Biscoe's father was a parson-squire, and lived at Kneesworth Hall near Cambridge. He was, too, a scholar of note, and taught Hebrew at the University. Biscoe, being a second son, had followed his father into the church. Happily, due to his father's patronage he had, at the time of his marriage to Mina, obtained the living of the nearby parish of Shepreth. Ten years later they moved to Devonshire, to a living in the gift of the Earl of Portsmouth, the remote and beautiful parish of Eggesford. Here it was, as soon as they arrived, that troubles arose which almost overwhelmed them.

Family affairs, and Robbie Ross

The first of these was the loss of Biscoe's allowance. Until then, every year, his father had given him £80, a small but certainly useful addition to his very meagre stipend at Shepreth. Quite suddenly his father stopped it, and announced he would never pay it again. Possibly Biscoe and Mina had annoyed him by moving away from the family circle although at the time, in the 1880s, a financial blizzard was sweeping the country – the summer of 1879 was the worst for more than sixty years – so the father's coffers may have been empty.

The next was the state of Eggesford Rectory. A plain, eighteenth-century villa with a slate roof and sash windows, it was badly in need of repairs and enlargement. Biscoe put the work in hand with a small builder from a nearby village, and then discovered he could not pay for it. His status as Lord Portsmouth's friend, not to speak of his rank as a clergyman which at first had given him credit, made his predicament all the worse. The builder waited as long as he could, and then gave Biscoe a final warning. The latter must pay within a week, or else be sued in the local court for bankruptcy.

A family crisis of this severity was felt, of course, by all its members. Biscoe needed £500; the bank had refused him further credit, and so had the fund for delapidations known as Queen Anne's Bounty. He just did not know where to turn; his father refused to answer his letters, and O.B. to whom he wrote (for whom a debt of £500 was more than the value of a year's Fellowship) was equally disinclined to help. Only Mrs Browning remained, who agreed to lend him £300, but all her money was still in stock in the Browning family business at Lewes, and thanks to Frederick's misdemeanours it was frozen in the hands of the family solicitor. On this account, O.B. was attacked as being the one who was really at fault. Mina wrote to him angrily, saying,

> . . . if the £300 is not forthcoming by next Wednesday week we shall be sold up & have to give up here & go I do not know where. Let me beg of you to take some active steps in the matter – of course you are alone responsible & if you give the order it can and must be

done – I have told you the alternative it is not exaggerated. I told you it would come to it at Xmas & I told Mama the same thing but she thought she was sure of her money before this. The builder has been to Lord Portsmouth's agent Mr. Thomas about it which is of course most unpleasant for us. If it were to come to his Lordship's ears I do not know what we should do. I entreat you to take action in the matter & do what in justice ought to have been done long since.[4]

Somehow or another the crisis was solved. Biscoe's father was made to relent, and the overdraft was guaranteed. Life at Eggesford settled down. Bills, however, mounted again, for Biscoe's stipend was quite inadequate. Children, too, began to appear: Philip, Oswald and Dorothea. Before very long, the Worthams found themselves in frightful difficulties a second time.

Once more the family was summoned, and once again by guarantees, the overdrafts were secured for the moment. 'Dick', O.B., and Mrs Browning were all now heavily involved. Yet again O.B. was attacked for his failure to deal with the family brewery; and, as always seems to happen when family affairs have gone astray, a passing thrust was given as well at the innocent family solicitor. 'The business should have been sold eighteen months ago', Mina told O.B. 'The longer it goes on, the more it deteriorates in value. The only one who profits in the matter is Mr. Nicholson who runs up long bills . . . I must say, I think it a pity you do not give up the trusteeship into more competent hands, when if the matter ever is settled, the estate will be swallowed up in law expenses which, I have no doubt is Mr. Nicholson's intention.'

O.B. was unrepentant. The trouble at Lewes had nothing to do with it, he told Mina in a tart reply. The responsibility was clearly Biscoe's who had no more moral sense than a foolish undergraduate.

For a short while some light relief came with a pupil called Binney. Many clergymen in those days boarded pupils to increase their incomes, and when the Worthams had been at Shepreth, only a mile or two from Cambridge, they had often done so without any trouble. When they moved to Eggesford, however, to find them proved to be almost impossible. Beautiful though the district was, with excellent fishing in the river Taw and fine hunting with the local hounds, they were more than twenty miles from Exeter, and in winter frequently quite cut off. Parents declined to send their boys there. If they did so, their sons detested it. Several times after the holidays boys who had been there refused to return with the consequent loss of fees to the Worthams. Binney, however, stuck it out, partly because he was very idle, and Biscoe more or less left him alone, and partly because he liked O.B. He came from Pampisford, close to Cambridge, and had met O.B. at the university. The latter had suddenly taken him up and promised to get him into King's – to which end he had sent him to Eggesford. He had also made him a pair of slippers (like many men, he liked embroidering), doubtless to guard against the draughts which must have whistled under the doors in the bitter, Devon winter months. Binney was frightfully pleased with the slippers and wrote that they were 'quite a masterpiece'. He used to write 'My Dear Doctor', and end his letters with 'Best Love', calling himself 'Your affec nate friend'. Binney, in fact, was one of his pets. He used to report on the Wortham household and on Biscoe's friendships with the Eggesford choirboys. Of all this Biscoe, of course, was ignorant.

Victorian parents were always spying, obsessed as they were with their children's purity, and Binney nearly got into trouble by not remembering this vital fact. Perhaps because his parents were dead, he was kept at Eggesford during the holidays, and he very unwisely wrote to a friend in terms which Biscoe afterwards reported to O.B.[5]

I ought to have added with regard to Binney, that I think his morals will need careful looking after at Cambridge. I don't know whether you have discovered anything about him on these points, but he wrote a letter to another boy whom I have here, in the holidays, inviting him 'to accompany him to the Westminster Aquarium where they could pick up a couple of women & enjoy themselves.' The boy to whom Binney wrote was staying in

London with his uncle, who somehow got hold of the letter, & told me of it a day or two ago when I met him at Torquay. *You must not tell Binney*, as I was told under promise of secrecy, and it would make mischief. Fortunately the boy did not respond, so there was no harm done, except in intention. I have not, of course, told Binney that I positively know of this, but have only given him general warning on these points.

Binney was twenty-one at the time, had known O.B. for several months, and hardly needed Biscoe's warning. The only lesson he must have learnt was to be more careful when writing letters to his friends.

Biscoe, too, had other worries. Once more, for the third time, the bills began to fall like snowflakes, and nothing he did allayed the blizzard. He realised, at last, he could not go on. All he could do was to write to O.B., implore his help for the last time, and take steps to make fresh arrangements. So once more, the family met, and 'Dick', O.B., and Biscoe's father deposited funds against the overdraft which now had risen to £500. 'I *simply cannot* pay the tradespeople', Biscoe told O.B. in a frantic letter. His credit had once again dried up; his stipend was only £140.

Quite suddenly he discovered the perfect solution to all their problems. His plan was to buy a boys' school in Bruges. The school he wanted was called 'Laurence's', and its annual profit was quite dramatic. After deducting all the expenses it netted almost a thousand pounds. The price was only two years' income, and this the vendor was ready to advance. What better proof could be had of the school's certain financial return than the vendor's readiness to lend against it?

Every other member of the family thought that the project was quite insane; in particular, O.B., who had no faith in Biscoe's ability even to teach the Eggesford choir boys. Already backing Biscoe's debts to the tune of almost a thousand pounds, he considered the scheme to be 'outrageous'. However, Biscoe went ahead. Of course, money was needed for the move; also, all the Eggesford tradesmen, as soon as they learnt that the

Worthams were leaving, immediately closed their books and submitted their bills.

At the last moment, to add to the problems, the vendor capriciously changed his mind. Biscoe had gone for a term of duty as deputy-head to smooth the transfer. He foolishly started to make some changes before he was properly able to do so, in particularly to ban caning, a form of rebuke he wholly disliked, except in cases of gross disobedience. The vendor, being still headmaster, felt his authority undermined. He seized the contract, tore it up, and ordered Biscoe off the premises.

Biscoe now heavily committed, financially, morally and practically too, having appointed a curate for Eggesford and moved his family over to Belgium, was forced to take the matter to court. For once, Fortune took his side. The judge awarded him handsome damages, more than the total cost of the school, and praised his lenient views on corporal punishment.

Biscoe sent delighted telegrams to 'Dick', O.B., and everyone else. Since the case had been in the papers and he wished to avoid the results of publicity, he changed the name of the school to 'The English College'. Safely far away from Eggesford and out of reach of rapacious creditors, it seemed at last that his troubles had come to an end.

Mrs Browning's death, however, in the summer of 1889, the year after he went to Bruges, led to the old, familiar problems. He had owed her more than £300, and now he found that he had to repay it. This he was quite unable to do. The school had not fulfilled its promise. On his arrival, the boys had mutinied. The number in prospect had fallen rapidly. The local bank had withdrawn its credit. He told O.B. – his mother's executor and also residuary legatee to whom, therefore, he owed the money – that the sole hope was to lend him more. Only the cancellation of the debt or another loan with which to pay it could solve the matter at the present hour. Hope is sometimes better than nothing. Biscoe could offer little else. For the seventh time in as many years, O.B. agreed to wait and back his overdraft.

In those days of rigorous morals a family's life was full of anxieties. From the hour a boy went to school to the day he was safely married in church, every sign of masturbation, every tender outside friendship, was checked by fathers, uncles, guardians, with stern, loving, Christian rectitude. Keys were taken from bathroom doors, sheets were checked for nightly emissions, even lavatories were kept open to avoid the tempting dangers of privacy. Thus it was at 'The English College'. Boys up to the age of twenty lived together, strictly supervised; all the more in need of care because of having to reside abroad amongst foreigners and Roman Catholics. It was, of course, taken for granted – indeed considered perfectly right – that Biscoe should, in certain circumstances, if he became at all suspicious, open a pupil's mail.

In October 1893, Biscoe began to suspect a boy called Dansey. He was 'nice looking, well mannered, a little over sixteen, of no particular strength of character.' Biscoe spied on Dansey's post and finally intercepted a letter which more than confirmed his worst suspicions. It revealed he had formed an immoral friendship with a prominent, young, literary aesthete.

Five years earlier, in 1888, Biscoe had actually met the latter staying with Mrs Browning in England. The aesthete had been an undergraduate – Robbie Ross, the friend of Wilde – and had just been ducked in the fountain at King's. O.B. had brought him down to Windsor. There, in the pure family home of Mrs Browning and 'Dick' at The Beehive, Biscoe had shaken Ross's hand and formally made his acquaintance. Much, much worse was to follow. Dansey's case was bad enough, but on discussing it with his son Philip, Biscoe discovered that he, too, had been seduced by Robbie Ross at that same weekend at Windsor.

Philip's own report was sent guilelessly to O.B. 'This is his statement,' Biscoe wrote, '& I give it in its naked hideousness.'

When I first knew Mr. Ross, at Windsor, at the Beehive in my grandmother's lifetime he behaved in an indecent manner. I was in his room alone with him early one morning, before breakfast. I was in my nightshirt, he was in his pyjamas: he put me on the bed. He had me between the legs. He placed his . . . between my legs. He did it on 3 occasions. When I was staying in London with him on a second occasion. The 3rd time was in his rooms at Church St. One time was at Christmas in London. It was when I was reading with Mr. Edwards. I went to London and spent the night there from Windsor.

'Such is Philip's statement,' Biscoe concluded, 'and at this time he must have been somewhere about 14.'

Biscoe, of course, was totally ignorant of the nature of O.B.'s relationship with Ross, of the merry weekend on the Isle of Wight with the 'fair sailor', Matthew Oates, which had taken place after Christmas, immediately after Philip's seduction.

So when the crisis with Dansey arose in October 1893 (at the very time, as it happened, that Matthew Oates had returned to London and begun to embarrass O.B. again) Biscoe wrote without reserve, little guessing that everything he said would be passed to Robbie Ross at once; and without the very least idea that O.B. liked young boys himself.

Absolute secrecy in this matter is essential for all [he warned O.B.]. Philip's name is not likely to come out. The events related happened some time ago & Ross has no letters of his . . . The details of the case of this boy here are too horrible. Ross is simply one of a gang of the most absolutely brutal ruffians who spend their time in seducing & prostituting boys & all the time presenting a decent appearance to the world. Two other persons besides himself are implicated in this business. Unfortunately there are some compromising letters which it is very desirable to get at.

I write to you in absolute secrecy to tell you what a scoundrel this fellow is, & he stayed with us only at Easter when he took the opportunity of our hospitality to make friends with this boy (a very nice looking gentlemanly boy of very good family of 16) whom he invited to London & seduced!!

Mina naturally wrote as well although her anxiety was slightly different. She was mostly worried about Oswald, her younger son, who was known as Toddy. He had always spoken highly of Ross, indeed called him his dearest friend. Biscoe had written to

11 The Senate House, OB's tricycle (?), and cabs, 1892

12 Clare, King's, and canoeing on the Backs

13 OB in old age by Emanuel Gliecenstein

Family affairs, and Robbie Ross

Toddy at once with a list of unambiguous questions. If Ross had corrupted Dansey at Easter, had he made love to Toddy as well? Much to Mina's and Biscoe's surprise, Ross suddenly arrived at Bruges. He had, of course, received an early warning from O.B.

My dear Oscar, [Mina wrote on October 16th] I have just received your letter & hasten to answer it by the last post. Biscoe was surprised last evening by a note from Mr. Ross asking for an interview at the Hotel de Flandre – with him was Lord Alfred Douglas, one of his accomplices. The fact is that there are some letters in the possession of Mr. Ross & Lord Alfred Douglas which must be had – if they would give them up, nothing would be done. Do you think you could get them. Sooner or later Biscoe thinks they will be in the hands of the police & then of course these compromising letters would be public property. I do intreat of you to get them. I am miserable about poor Toddy. Of course I have no idea what his relations are with Mr. Ross now. Up to the last few days I looked upon Mr. Ross as Toddy's valued friend & I wrote to Mr. Ross last summer & told him how much I valued his friendship for the 2 boys. Biscoe has written a string of questions to Toddy but there is no answer from him – he might well have written – What effect these questions may have had I cannot tell – anyhow, if he has written any letters to Mr. Ross, they must be had. I wish you could see Toddy. Biscoe, nor the father of the boy lately compromised have any intention of taking criminal proceedings, in fact nothing can be done excepting to get any letters & prevent any more intercourse with Mr. Ross. My idea is that you could get them better than any one else. I am so distressed about Toddy's position because he is away & of course knows nothing excepting the questions Biscoe has put to him. I am quite distressed about the boy & think I shall go to England & see him. If he has written any letters they *must* be given up. I am afraid I have written an inconsequent sort of letter but I am so bothered & troubled I hardly know what I am about. You *may* be quite sure that no proceedings will be taken, of course Biscoe feels as you do, that the reputation of the whole family is at stake.

The moment Ross had seen Biscoe, he wrote a report to O.B.[6]

Family affairs, and Robbie Ross

Grand Hotel du Phare
Ostende
October 16th 1893

Dear Mr Browning

Following your advice I came out here yesterday morning & went over to Bruges in the evening & had an interview with Mr. Wortham at the Hotel de Flandre. It was very unsatisfactory. He refuses to tell me what he proposes doing. He says he possesses documentary evidence but what he intends doing with this (if it exists) he will not say. He also speaks of 'coming to terms' but does not state what those terms are beyond the fact that I have certain letters from the boy Dansey which I must hand over. He will not tell me which letters they are. I have no letters from him that could not be read in public. I therefore write to ask you to ascertain from Mr. Wortham 1st What he means by coming to terms. 2nd what he proposes doing if we do not come to terms. Of course I shall know sooner or later but it would materially assist me & everyone concerned if I knew at once. I was also confronted with Philip who repeated his story. It is an absolute fabrication. If it were true I certainly would not attempt to conceal it from *you*, as you must know perfectly well. From what you have often told me about Mr. Wortham & what *you know yourself* about him it is in your power to free the whole affair of its more serious aspects without compromising yourself in any way.

Sincerely yours, R.B. Ross

In reply please write to 24 Thornton Street, Kensington, W.

The Dansey crisis came to an end thanks to O.B.'s role as a double agent. 'My dear Oscar,' Biscoe wrote on 25th October. 'At length I am thankful to say we have got to the end of this dreadful case. The letters have been returned on both sides, and now one feels relieved of a nightmare . . . It has been a *horrible case*, & the details, which I have, and am the only one who knows except the chief actors in the business are beyond everything abominable. We may be thankful that it has ended quietly, but it has been a near thing.'

Mina wrote to O.B., too, for once beginning 'My dearest Oscar,' and ending with the words, 'yours affectionately'. Her own concern – the purity of Toddy – had been established without a doubt. He had never done anything wrong with Ross, and had answered all his father's questions to his parents' perfect satisfaction. O.B. could have told them otherwise. He had heard privately from More Adey, the third member of Ross's gang, that Toddy's letters had all been burnt. Mina, of course, knew nothing of this. As a clergyman's wife she studied her Bible, and liked to spice her letters with quotations. 'I feel like a roe in the mountains', she wrote, thinking perhaps of the Song of Solomon but not getting the phrase quite right. Then aged fifty-one, and long suffering from overweight, her sense of relief is well conveyed in spite of the metaphor's slight unsuitability.

Biscoe's time at 'The English College' had now almost come to an end. Few schools at that period could survive the suspicion of immorality, and although, of course, everyone concerned did their best to conceal the drama, rumours began to get about, and the number of pupils dwindled steadily. By the summer of 1896, eight years after he arrived, Biscoe decided to give it up. He had then only twelve boarders, having begun with sixty-nine. The fact was, he was quite incapable either of managing a school or of making money.

Once again he was faced with the problem of where to go to make a living. He sold the College, returned to England, and just survived as a *locum tenens* until at last, in 1902, he was made the rector of Ware in Hertfordshire. Here, in the summer of 1904, occurred his last and worst disaster. He was charged with 'certain improper acts' with a young cowherd called David Wilkinson – a 'filthy charge' as the newspapers said – and taken off to Brixton Prison. It proved a case of mistaken identity, but local feeling ran high, there were ugly rumours about the choir boys, Biscoe was beaten up in the street, and had to be taken away by the Bishop.

The unhappy Mina packed again. She told O.B. all about it. It was, she said, her hand trembling, their seventeenth move in six years.

CHAPTER XI

'Well and fat and not too amorous'

If all these frightful crises were taking place in O.B.'s family and occupying much of his time, other dramas, just as fearful, were using up his energy and thoughts in the dangerous world of his homosexual acquaintances.

By far the most traumatic of these was the trial and conviction of Oscar Wilde. In May 1895 he was sent to prison for 'gross indecency'. The entire homosexual brotherhood – all but Wilde's intimate friends – were aghast at what came out in the proceedings. All those like O.B. who, perhaps, once in a while, committed acts which broke the law but who in general preferred merely to talk and cuddle, to write verses about Greek Love, to boggle at boys in the Turkish baths, to pore over photographs of youths, posed naked in 'Greek' attitudes, were deeply shocked by Wilde's behaviour.

A number of letters in the Browning archive, mostly from men who had known Wilde, if only casually like O.B., but all with homosexual interests, make this point conclusively. An old pupil, William Paton, known as 'Poodle' to his Eton friends, author of a book on the island of Cos whose youths were famous for their feminine beauty, wrote in 1897,[1]

You already, I think, know that this catastrophe was a personal catastrophe for myself, because it so happened that his best friend, his marriage trustee, was is my best friend & I used whenever I went to London to have the inestimable privilege of hearing Oscar Wilde talk to us very intimately every day. Needless to say that although my friend & I were aware of his penchant for young men (notably Lord A.D.) & of his extreme imprudence in expressing his adoration we were ignorant of his excesses, which he unluckily concealed from us.

Oscar Wilde, as you will have heard, has returned to his vomit. It is tragic & too horrible. I know it *almost directly from his wife*. I abandon him. You know my sentiments & I know yours.

'Well and fat and not too amorous'

Nine years later R.C. Jackson, the eccentric poet and, according to himself, the original Marius of Walter Pater's *Marius the Epicurean* wrote[2]

> My beloved Browning, today I lunched with Mr. Ross . . . & he made terrible things known to me, respecting the person we spoke about . . . The while *he* gave myself information which saved linking my name with such a foul and detestable person – he appeared to think nothing of such foul enormities, saying 'Michael Angelo, Shakespeare, J.A. Symonds, Pater & many others were equally admirers of the same sort of thing' – that was *his* excuse to me: when I with indignation told him I would not publish a single line with respect to O.W. When he mentioned Pater's name (saying the same was well known to Professor Jowett) I tackled him upon that matter & MADE HIM give me his authority for such an assertion – when he said Simeon Solomon told him so.

O.B. had letters, too, on the same subject from Frank Money, another minor poet. He wrote eclectic verse about love which was understood by all the initiates to be of the kind that was known as 'Uranian'. An Old Etonian, like 'Poodle' Paton, he had often met Wilde socially. Money's feelings were more humane, ones of simple regret at such a disaster. 'Oscar W's business sickens me', he wrote shortly before the former's imprisonment, 'not with Pharisaic sentiment, but at the waste and premature entombment of genius.' Again, a fortnight later, on the 22nd April 1895, 'O. Wilde's case is miserable. Such wasted talent. My belief is that he *deliberately* went in for depraved excitement.'

O.B.'s part in Wilde's tragedy was confined to helping to pay his debts. Robbie Ross, staying with More Adey in Gloucestershire, wrote in October 1895,[3]

> I venture to write & ask you whether you would be willing or able to subscribe to the sum which is being collected to annul the bankruptcy proceedings against Oscar Wilde . . . Of the £2000 required £1500 has already been collected from friends & several strangers who have generously contributed.

139

'Well and fat and not too amorous'

The proposal to avert the bankruptcy may at first seem quixotic but it is only because the reasons are many that Oscar Wilde's friends have decided to do so. Among them I may mention the following . . . To spare him the further pain of a public examination & for one who has already endured such terrible suffering this means a great deal. Utterly broken in health & spirit he told a friend who was privileged to see him not long ago that he dreaded the examination in bankruptcy more than anything he had gone through.

No names of subscribers will be *made public* so none of the charitably disposed need fear lest the appearance of their names might give the impression that they were in any way connected with Oscar Wilde or sympathised with him except as one who has suffered & will suffer for the next two years the most terrible & cruel torture known to English injustice & Anglo Saxon hypocrisy.

In the end the bankruptcy went ahead, the debt becoming too great for Wilde's friends to be able to meet it. Those who had tried to help were refunded. A note in the file from Wilde's solicitor showed that O.B. had sent him six pounds. Wilde did not forget his kindness. On release from prison he went to Paris and sent O.B., via Robbie Ross, a copy of his bitter, dramatic poem, 'The Ballad of Reading Gaol'.

An obsessive pursuit is as blind as love. O.B.'s passion for boys, in spite of the dangers of such encounters – blackmail, syphilis, even imprisonment – continued with unabated delight, both in London and at Cambridge. 'Look, look, how Coan that is!' O.B. cried out one day when he saw a boy in shorts and singlet, wet to the skin from falling in a brook, showing his lithe and manly outline. In Roman times the island of Cos was famous for 'Coan vestments' – very light, transparent garments. Arthur Benson at the University witnessed this particular incident and recorded his shock and disgust in his diary.[4] The boy was on a hare & hounds run along the Barton Road and O.B. had pedalled out on his tricycle to see it 'because it was so Greek'.

In London, thanks to Frank Money who gave him £100 a year, O.B. was able to pursue these interests with equal avidity.

'Well and fat and not too amorous'

Frank Money made this gift because he really loved O.B. with a love that had never flinched or faded since he had been a devoted pupil at Eton. In later years extremely rich, he was able to give O.B. an allowance simply in the name of their old friendship. Nothing anyone ever did gave O.B. more freedom or satisfaction. With this sum he rented a set of chambers at 88 St James's Street. Here he could go whenever he liked, and entertain his friends as he pleased, without anybody asking questions. The location also was very convenient, directly beside St James's Palace. It was near his club, the Athenaeum; five minutes' walk from Buckingham Palace; close to most of the galleries and theatres; a stone's throw from the Turkish Baths. So the rooms served all his interests: his learned studies; his social ambitions; his artistic pursuits; his sexual fantasies. They were altogether quiet and private. Mrs Chilcott, the obliging housekeeper, lit the fires, made the beds, paid the bills, and never appeared – so long as she received her wages.

An unusual mixture of friends and acquaintances came and went at '88'. There were valets, choristers and undergraduates; engineers and bath attendants; boys from Borstal, clowns and crossing sweepers. Any youth whom O.B. liked, to whom he thought he could do a kindness, perhaps in exchange for a little amusement, arrived, stayed and went away, sometimes never to be seen again, occasionally to ring the bell too often.

There was George Bailey, a 'good shampooer'; John Barker who was 'big and strong'; Hermann Stellmann, a Swiss hairdresser; Charles Kummer, a Soho waiter; Sidney Bliss who went to prison; Sewell Ambrose, a factory apprentice, who was 'well & fat & not *too amorous*'. There was William Campbell, 'Little Billie' a youth who was actually twenty-one, who came one morning at 4 a.m. to find O.B. was not at home, his bedroom occupied by four boys, two to a bed in each other's arms. There was Wallace Sutcliffe who promised to stay but then, suddenly, cancelled by telegram. He explained afterwards that 'certain particulars', unexpectedly learnt from a friend, particularly 'painful to me in themselves', had made it advisable not to see him. There were aristocratic visitors, too, like Lord Ronald

Sutherland-Gower, the fourth son of the Duke of Sutherland, the model for Lord Henry Wotton in Wilde's *Picture of Dorian Gray*. He promised O.B. a treat from Denmark. 'Two charming youths', he described them. 'One a Baron Rosenkrantz – I suppose a descendant of Hamlet's friend?' There was also a boy called Freddie Campbell, an Old Etonian who went insane. He began to behave in a 'violent manner', strangled his dog, attacked the maid, and had to be taken off to a home. He wrote some incoherent letters which O.B. ought to have thrown away.[5]

> Yesterday morning your angelic divine – What – you remember I met him at your dinner party – left us . . . I stood on the top of the station bridge till the last adorable back of the last adorable carriage of the adorable train that comprised the unthinkably adorable compartment which contained his adorable self had disappeared round a curve . . . I must really thank you though dear O.B. for having been the means of procuring [scored out] introducing me to so very desirable an acquaintance . . .

His doctor wrote O.B. a note. He gave him some very welcome advice. Campbell ought to be left alone. He did not think it a good idea for O.B. to go and see him.

On many occasions with difficult boys, O.B. found that such counsel was easier to give than to follow. Although he invariably tired of his protégés – it was only a matter of time – he nearly always had fearful trouble in managing to see them less and less, and finally in getting rid of them. This was especially so in London where the great convenience of '88' being close to many of his friends, also put him at a disadvantage. At King's, if he wished to be alone, he could tell the porter he was not at home, go to his rooms and be left in peace. In St James's Street, it was much more difficult. He was likely to meet his friends on the doorstep. On some occasions at '88', it must have seemed to Mrs Chilcott as she answered the door bell yet again, very often late at night, that she lived in a house that was almost in a state of siege.

Two boys in particular, Willie Barrable and Featonby Smith simply would not be shouldered off; and in each case their numerous letters (from Willie Barrable, ninety-one; from Smith, one hundred and forty-seven) provide an extraordinarily vivid picture of the rise and fall of an O.B. passion.

Willie Barrable was fifteen when he first fell in with O.B. and he seems, for reasons not clear, to have lodged in O.B.'s rooms at King's, perhaps in the role of a junior secretary. The first letter in the correspondence, of June 1896, begins 'Dear Mr. Browning' so at this date it is quite evident that the affair was only just beginning. Willie had recently been left alone – O.B. had gone to '88' – so Willie was feeling the pangs of parting. Although still writing formally as a boy would to an older man – O.B. was fifty-nine – he did close with 'fondest love'. He found it hard to express his emotions. O.B.'s love had been overwhelming. 'I miss you extremely in the mornings when I get up & go out to bathe by myself,' he said.[6] 'You can't tell with what joy I take up my pen to write a few words to you . . . I have got your photo on a table beside the bed & that cheers me up a great deal, in fact I couldn't do without it being there . . . it seems to me that you are "pres de moi".'

Not wishing to deny his father whom he loved dearly also, but longing to place O.B. in a close family relationship, a few days later he subscribed himself 'your affectionate Grandson'. He had just got into long trousers, he told O.B. in a glow of happiness. He wrote again the following day, the fifth loving letter within a fortnight.

The next parting which provoked letters happened a month later during August. O.B. had taken Willie to Holland, and then gone on to Germany. A whole week alone together, spent sightseeing in Rotterdam, gave Willie a sum of happiness such as he never had hoped to experience. His only holidays in the past had been to Devonshire to stay with his grandfather who earned his living as a family ironmonger.

My dearest friend Mr. Browning [Willie wrote on board ship as it pitched and yawed back to Harwich], I do miss you, you can't tell how much, & in thinking of you this morning, I nearly shed 'lacrimas'. I used to feel so joyful when you was in my company, that now I feel 'tam desertus'. But I must try & be as joyful as I can. You are *nearly* the same as a father to me. I love you still more, now I am 'non tecum'. I love to think of you, & your joyful jokes, but (alas) I shall not see your lovely face for 2 whole months. Alas! what a time that will be to me. It will seem more like two years 'tu carissimas hominorum'. You must excuse my kind of letter, as the emotion of my heart concerning you is more than you can contemplate. Ever, ever, your most affectionate friend Willie.

Willie fell ill shortly afterwards, and his father agreed to answer for him in case he was infectious. His father was clearly a plain man, simply grateful for O.B.'s attentions, unaware of his reputation, or the possibility of sexual interest. He wrote from Devonshire,

Dear Sir, In the first place I deeply regret to inform you that Wm. is ill with Scarletina . . . Dr. Deighton says it is a very mild case, in fact he said Wm. might get up on the 8th day and have a bath and he gets up every day since at 7 or 8 bells. My wife tells me that he keeps on asking for you everytime she takes him anything, she says he worries 50 times more because he can't write to you than he does of being ill and she has not the slightest doubt there is the most intense love and affection in his heart for you. Not long since she tells me she asked him who he loved best, his reply was, I love Mr. Browning, when she pressed the question a little further and he replied, Mr. Browning is my best and dearest friend I do love Mr. Browning. And really one cannot be surprised after such kindness. I hear he is going on *well* and I hope to return in a day or two when I will write you again and let you know how he is. Thank you most sincerely for all your kindness to him,
    I remain dear Sir, Your very Obedient Servant, Wm. Hy. Barrable

In this manner two years passed, Willie remaining deeply in love and O.B. quietly biding his time. During the term they bathed together, and during the holidays went abroad, once to Mainz and once to Rome. Willie, of course, went home at times. When left alone, he continued to write – long, innocent, boyish letters – which as he grew, turned more serious and turned, also, much more boring. 'Mr. Browning' became 'O.B.'. 'My ever dearest O.B., I miss you dreadfully', he said in one of them, going on to discuss the weather, the books he had read and his constipation. Although aged seventeen, he still remained entirely ignorant of O.B.'s real desires and intentions. Then at last he left school. Thanks to O.B.'s intercession, he got a job as a clerk in the Bank of England.

Whatever happened in the next months, whatever pederasts he may have met (one, certainly, was George Ives, a secretive, well-known homosexual), whatever took place at '88', at the end of a year a break occurred, and Willie was suddenly, painfully rejected. One has to assume that at long last O.B. attempted an initiation and that poor Willie who was quite innocent, and also rather inclined to be religious, escaped in a state of shock and disgust. Then, in spite of every advance, every attempt to renew the friendship on which so much of his spirit depended, every plea for restoration of the old, happy 'grandfather' relationship, he failed to achieve a reconciliation. He was cast out and left to himself. Instead of love, he received long letters of recrimination.

Another of O.B.'s little friends with whom he, at the same time, was having an extended passionate courtship, and who was also a clerk in the Bank of England, gave O.B. the satisfaction of hearing how deeply his blows had cut. 'Poor Willie Barrable', he told O.B. in a letter written after the break. 'I can't understand him at all, he seems full of all sorts of troubles. I am awfully sorry for him. I was with him a long time on Monday night & had a long talk with him. He says I cannot understand his quarrel with you . . . what he means I don't know . . . I met Geo. Ives in the Strand last night. It seems that poor Willie B. has offended him too.' This correspondent was Featonby Smith. In less than a year the cause of Barrable's grief was to seem unpleasantly clear to him.

O.B.'s affair with Featonby Smith began, so far as Smith was concerned, with delightful unexpectedness. He met O.B. in 1889, in what circumstances is not clear. His father had suffered financial losses, and shortly after O.B. appeared, was asking

O.B.'s advice on how to earn a living as a schoolmaster. Perhaps he had written, as many did, out of the blue and without introduction, to ask for O.B.'s advice and help.

Featonby Smith was a clerk in the City. As soon as he and O.B. had met, and as soon as O.B. had got his address, a multitude of favours was showered upon him. Although the same age as Barrable, seventeen at the time of the meeting, and in some ways just as innocent, in other ways it seems clear that he played the part that O.B. desired, whatever exactly that might be, from the very early days of their relationship.

His first letter is full of simplicity. O.B. had taken him to the zoo. He wrote like the good boy he was – he had been the Head of Eye Grammar School – to thank O.B. for a happy day. He still could not believe his luck. 'I hardly know how to thank you enough', he said, 'it is awfully good of you to take such an interest in me so suddenly.'

This was on Thursday October 10th. Three days later he received a photograph. He thanked O.B. and promised to reciprocate. By the 25th he had been initiated, and told O.B.'s most personal secret. O.B., it seems, had a growth on his foreskin which was making the end of his penis painful. Smith consulted a friend and room-mate, a medical student called Edgar Simpson. With all of a budding surgeon's authority, the latter advised an immediate circumcision.

No letters in the Browning Archive point more clearly than Edgar Simpson's to O.B.'s homosexuality, to his love of flirting with his own kind, to his dangerous fancy for charming youth, to his pederastic delights and experiments. Whether or not he committed sodomy with Featonby Smith or anybody else (and wart-like growths on the male organ are commonly caused by such activities), no man of sixty-one would discuss such matters with young clerks, boys he had only lately met, lads of seventeen, unless he desired a sexual relationship, if only one of prurient excitement. Perhaps this was all he dared; perhaps lascivious talk aroused him; perhaps he could not do anything else, and this was his real problem. Certainly he did not desist from intimate contact for legal, moral or religious motives. If he drew back from consummation, perhaps he did so against his will: for the one simple, embarrassing reason that when the exciting moment came, his manly ability left him.

Smith and Simpson had their rewards. A dazzling shower of gifts arrived at Munich House, their 'diggings' close to Regent's Park, turkeys and champagne, bottles of claret and tickets to the theatre. Smith was given a dress suit, a 'magnificent desk with secret drawers', and a splendid gold watch and chain. There was even a present for Smith's brother who was still only a small boy. O.B. sent him an army of toy soldiers of all ranks with all their equipment. Smith and Simpson must have smiled, and accused O.B. when he came to supper, of teaching Georgie before his time, how to sit on the floor and 'play with his privates'.

Smith's downfall came suddenly, due to a series of personal calamities. He fell in love with a girl called Ina, and never dared to tell O.B. until he had formally become engaged. Immediately he received a stern letter, advising him to change his mind at once. Smith, to his credit, refused to comply, so he found himself abruptly dismissed, his presence and letters no longer accepted. Then he began to get into trouble. He lost his post in the Bank of England for returning late after his honeymoon. In a few weeks he needed money. He had no one to turn to except O.B. who had often said, as he usually did to all the different boys he befriended, that if in want they must always approach him. Smith did so in long letters, begging a loan of eighty pounds. Of course, O.B. never sent it, such a sum being far too great, even to lend to a member of his family. Smith soon was in desperate straits. He wrote to O.B. again and again, telling a story that every week was more and more pathetic and disastrous. The rent was due; Ina was ill; worst of all, she was having a baby. His letters were sadly similar to Biscoe's. He wrote on January 12th from Alf Cooke's Office, Oswaldstone Ho., Norfolk St., Strand,[7]

My dear O.B., I *must* have £10 tomorrow, do help me this once. Do lend it to me & I shall try and repay in a week or two. It is hard work for me to keep afloat and recover lost ground at the same time, but I am doing it slowly.

I am trying my hardest to keep all expenses down & get straight, & I am doing so slowly. I must pay away £10 tomorrow Tuesday. My dear O.B. do lend it to me for pitys sake. Telegraph it to me that I may get it tomorrow. Do help me this once. I am sure you shall never regret it.

My dear O.B. do lend me the £10 for mercys sake & let me have it tomorrow.

Yours affectionately, F. Stafford Smith.

Such letters had arrived before. O.B. in fact, was thoroughly used to them. He passed it to Fred, his current secretary. The latter no doubt gave a discreet smile, and quietly, efficiently, filed it and locked it away.

CHAPTER XII

The paedagogue seeks the Holy Grail

Other letters filed by Fred in these years of private troubles at the turn of the century, came from a wide variety of sources and reveal O.B. in a different light entirely. Gone is the secret homosexual: instead O.B. stands as the figure he wished to be, the busy don and successful scholar, a paedagogue still at the height of his powers, a vigorous leading light in his field at Cambridge.

His output was enormous. He wrote, taught, lectured, corresponded with an almost inexhaustible energy. Although he had failed in the academic world – the Provostship of King's had gone to Austen Leigh; the Vice Provostship to Fred Whitting; even the Chair of History at Edinburgh to George Prothero, a younger colleague – his morale remained at its very highest. Except in the secret depths of his mind when, because of his chronic insomnia, he lay awake in the middle of the night and saw his life as it really was, a life of promise frittered away, he believed his career a real success, his public achievements unsurpassed. For beyond his ordinary donnish duties, the daily round of study and tuition, the weekly attendance on various committees, he had taken on an additional task. This was the training of elementary schoolmasters in a newly established Teaching College.

In this work he became absorbed. All hope of preferment abandoned, all family difficulties solved, all sexual excursions forgotten, he found success and recognition in this work until he retired. In it he saw his Holy Grail, the achievement, after fifty years, of his deepest personal ambition.

O.B.'s interest in paedagogics, which means the science and principles of teaching, began in the early 1860s when, as a young 'beak' at Eton, newly recruited from King's College, he found himself in charge of a 'Division', that is to say, a class of eighty boys. He had no previous training at all. Some could be had for elementary teaching but none whatever for secondary work. However, he settled down at once, perfectly sure that common sense and his own superior education would make the task interesting and simple. Soon he realised he had much to learn. With other inexperienced masters who had returned to their schools from Cambridge and found themselves in a similar position, he formed a club, the United Ushers. It met two or three times a year to hear a paper and hold a discussion.

The agenda for one of these meetings has survived, J.M. Wilson (later headmaster of Clifton College) reading the paper on the subject of 'Immorality in Schools'. O.B. doubtless spoke as well, for the Secretary (his old friend, Arthur Sidgwick) wrote a note on his agenda saying how much he hoped he would come. 'There is one point of view that no one will put as you could, & it ought to be put', he told him.[1] It is clear therefore that even then, in the first years of his mastership at Eton, his paederastic leanings were known, at least within his own circle. So his views on love as a force in the classroom as well as those on paedagogics were sought already, by those who knew him, with honest concern and respect.

O.B.'s ideas on education, most of all on the need for teachers to be taught theory as well as practice, had been put to use by the University very soon after he returned – after his sudden dismissal from his house at Eton. For several years the idea had been canvassed that some sort of teacher training ought to be given by Oxford and Cambridge for those planning to teach in secondary schools. Early in 1878, the latter decided to ask the opinion of one hundred and fifty people, mainly the Heads of Public Schools, who were closely connected with education. For this purpose a Syndicate was formed of which O.B. was made the Secretary. This gave him the ironic pleasure of having to write, among others, to Dr Hornby.

Hornby's reply must have delighted him. 'I should earnestly deprecate the Foundation of Professorships or Lectureships with a view to the training of young teachers', Hornby wrote.[2] It was just the negative view that O.B. had expected. 'Decidedly unfavourable', O.B. noted against Hornby's name in a *précis* he wrote for the Syndicate. On balance, however, the answers were encouraging. Twenty-four distinguished people, headed by Dr Jex-Blake, the very successful Headmaster of Rugby, were fully in favour of further experiment. A new committee was then set up in 1879 of which O.B. was again the Secretary: the Cambridge Teachers' Training Syndicate. It arranged lectures, held examinations, and each year awarded certificates on the 'theory, history and practice of Education' for those students, men and women, who were planning to teach in higher, or secondary schools.

More important than this, however, in the days before the University founded O.B.'s teaching college, it gave O.B. an official position in the field of education. As Secretary of the Cambridge Teachers' Syndicate, a post he held for thirty years, he was put in touch with the world at large and given something he badly needed, especially after the row with Hornby: a name and status outside the University. Now people began to write to him from all parts of the United Kingdom; and as the subject of education became more and more a public issue (universal education was one of the major topics of the day) and as the training of teachers progressed and acquired an increasing amount of support, he found himself at the hub of a network that stretched across the scholastic world. There were other people similarly placed; other secretaries of other committees in other centres of education who held appointments equivalent to his; but his personal renown and boundless energy placed him and kept him ahead of everyone.

The volume of mail that arrived at King's soon became enormous. In six months of a single year it amounted to more than six hundred letters. O.B. tirelessly dealt with them all. In a short while his famous initials, as well as being synonymous in Cambridge with social life and patronage of youth, also stood abroad, in Europe, America, even Japan, for the theory and practice of education. It was only natural that when, in 1891 the Senate decided to support a college for the day-training of elementary teachers, the Cambridge Teachers' Training

151

Syndicate under whose authority it came should ask O.B. to accept the post of Principal.

The Cambridge University Day Training College, to quote its comprehensive title, was one of a dozen similar colleges which came into being in the early 1890s. In 1880, elementary education had at last become obligatory for all children from the age of five; and one immediate consequence had been that more schools had been established, and more teachers had been required for them. Staff had then been hard to find, for at that time the career of a teacher, especially that of a village schoolmaster, was very far from being desirable. It provided only a meagre salary, held an inferior social position, and except in very special cases, appealed only to a humble few who were themselves imperfectly educated.

This fact had long been deplored, and for many years successive governments through a special committee of the Privy Council had done their best with grants and subsidies to make the profession more attractive. In particular, in 1846, Queen's Scholarships had been inaugurated to assist apprenticed pupil-teachers to study in religious teaching colleges. The scholarship scheme had been a success and had steadily raised the number and quality of those wishing to enter the profession; but the marked increase in elementary schools caused by the Act of 1880, and the consequent demand for primary teachers, led to renewed problems of staffing.

Government-sponsored day-training colleges in association with universities had been proposed as one of the methods by which to improve the situation. Thus it was that such an establishment came to be founded at the University of Cambridge. The early history of the Cambridge college is full of interest to anyone now who considers the University Department, its present day direct successor, with its two hundred graduate students all training for a further year to take a Certificate in Education, taught by a Professor and twenty Lecturers in the very manner that Dr Hornby deprecated. Happily for those who wish to study it, some account of these early days may be found in the annual Inspectors' Reports in

The paedagogue seeks the Holy Grail

the Ministry of Education Library.

Like all other day-colleges, of which there were soon to be fifteen in the major cities of England and Wales, the Cambridge college had a settled framework, carefully devised by the government office, known as the Department of Education, under whose direction it lay. It was planned to cater for twenty-five students, all of whom had to matriculate, that is to say, become undergraduates – registered members of the university. They could do so by joining an existing college: many, for example, went to King's. Or they could register as Non-Collegiate. They might live at home or stay in lodgings, but all were obliged to read for a degree as well as for their Government Teacher's Certificate. This entailed a tremendous effort, for the work had to be done concurrently within a period of three years. It included subjects like Scholastic Method, and practical work with children in the classroom, as well as the normal degree curriculum.

Many people had grave doubts about whether the students could possibly manage. Another problem also faced them. They had to pass the Previous Exam, the first test of the degree year, for which they needed Latin and Greek. The students attending the Day Training College had never done Latin or Greek in their lives for they all came from humble homes and most had been to elementary schools in which these languages had not been taught. The advantage of having a degree, however, was so great that most learnt them and passed this first hurdle successfully. In addition to which, instead of a pass, many decided from the very start to take the harder course and read for honours. In this they had to thank O.B. who encouraged them all to aim for the highest.

The whole idea of day-training, authorised by Parliament in 1890, was, itself, a bold experiment which proved to be, in later years (and partly due to O.B.'s enthusiasm) a milestone in the history of education. Until that time, teacher training had been undertaken in church colleges to which, with the aid of Queen's Scholarships, pupil-teachers from elementary schools had been encouraged to seek admission. Often called Normal Schools

153

The paedagogue seeks the Holy Grail

(from the French *Ecoles Normales*) the colleges had all been residential. This had proved a serious defect in the training of those who later on were to spend their lives as village schoolmasters; for three years of cloistered life, side by side with social superiors whose fees were being paid by parents, made them sensitive and supercilious. They were crammed with data for examinations for the government teacher's 'parchment certificate', but were widely deficient in general knowledge.

So day-colleges which were only open to Queen's Scholars were established within the universities. The hope was expressed and indeed fulfilled that the wider educational life and the greater freedom of non-residence would enable the students to start their careers not only with heads that were filled with facts, but also with hearts that were open to the world, and thus with minds that were widely cultivated.

O.B.'s theory of education which he arrived at in the early days at Eton and never changed throughout his life was exactly suited to these boys, the pupil-teacher Queen's Scholars who came to his Day Training College. Unconcerned with their physical charms since his sexual life was fulfilled in London, he was able to get to know them well and to forge a mutual bond of friendship without the distraction of wanting to kiss them. There are no letters in the Browning archive of a sexual nature from any of his pupils. He discovered their interests and fired their enthusiasms in just the way he thought the best: by frequent contact and private tutorial. This he believed was the only manner in which instruction ought to be given. If it failed in one direction, then it ought to be tried in another; for he felt convinced that every boy, whether from working background or not, had just as great a scholastic potential as the products of the middle and upper classes. In this he was far ahead of his time. He often said that a nation's greatness should be judged by the cost of its education: a point of view that is current today, a hundred years after he propounded it. Some of his swans turned out to be geese, but his passionate belief in a student's ability always produced the maximum effort. In the common phrase, he was a 'born teacher'; and every arrival in the new college soon acknowledged that this was really true. Like many projects, the Day Training College, the D.T.C. as it used to be called, started off extremely simply. It had no premises, no money and, apart from O.B. himself, only two part-time staff. It opened with only three students, in October 1891. The first to arrive was H.G. Wilson who wrote many years afterwards of his vivid memory of O.B., excitedly taking hold of his arm and rolling him rapidly to Parker's Piece to get him installed in his first lodgings. Wilson took his degree successfully, and so did his classmates, Stream and Delahunt. O.B. tutored them all proudly. He did so weekly in his rooms, sometimes while he was taking a bath. He, too, looking back, recalled those early days nostalgically. He said in his *Memories of Sixty Years* that being with them had been a 'pure delight'.

The annual reports of the government Inspectors who came round in these years to examine the practical work of the students, indicate how the college grew and prove that O.B.'s claims of success, always characteristically flamboyant, here were not exaggerated.

The numbers rose from the first three to twenty-two, three years later; and Mr Oakeley, the visiting Inspector, had 'every reason to be contented'. 'Very creditable progress', he wrote, after his next annual inspection. Six years afterwards in 1900 a new Inspector, Mr Currey, gave the college the following commendation.[3]

This college continues to increase in numbers and efficiency, but more rapidly in efficiency than numbers. There are 23 students – 6 first year, 9 second year, 8 third year. The majority of these are the holders of scholarships from Toynbee Hall. They are doing well both as regards professional training and University studies. They live the life of the University and a great personal interest in their comfort and welfare is taken by the Committee. Since last year a Common Room and a Lecture Room have been provided by the kindness of Mr. Oscar Browning. Mr. Iliffe, who is leaving, has shown himself a skilful master of method, and has not spared himself in the work. The practical work of the students seems to be quite as good as that produced in the Residential Colleges.

The paedagogue seeks the Holy Grail

Mr Iliffe, the Master of Method, the master, that is, who taught teaching became the cause of a violent conflict between O.B. and Miss Hughes who ran a Normal School for mistresses, the Cambridge Training College for Women, of which O.B. was always jealous. The storm itself was not important, and was brought about by a comment by Miss Hughes – an implied criticism of O.B. – which Iliffe carelessly reported back. O.B., always alert to the slightest criticism of any kind, but especially about his D.T.C., wrote Miss Hughes a furious letter. It reveals better than any Report how proud he was of his students' progress, and how deeply he felt that his work was of vital importance.[4]

My Dear Madam, the Cambridge University Day Training College is admitted by all who know anything about it to be not only a great but a most remarkable success. It was predicted when it was first started, one, that it would consist mainly of Cambridge residents, two, that the students would all be Non Collegiate, three, that they would not mix with the life of the University, four, that they would all be Normal men, five, that the college could not be carried on without a large sum of money. All these predictions have been falsified. There are very few (Cambridge) residents in the college and very few N.C. The students pass excellent examinations in their professional subjects and also take high honour degrees. They mix to the full in the undergraduate life of the place, and owing to the self-denial of the teaching staff the college is entirely self supporting. I enclose our two last reports in support of my assertions. The success of such an important experiment as ours ought to delight the heart of anyone who is interested in either the training of teachers or in the progress of education.

When Iliffe retired as Master of Method his place was taken by a Dr Sigmund Fechheimer. The latter's appointment was very important, not only because he taught well – he came from Rein's Academy at Jena – but also because with another master, he lived in a house which belonged to the College, Warkworth House, by Parker's Piece, and was thus directly in contact with all the students. Better still – or perhaps worse – he was also in contact with O.B. every single minute of the day, either in person or by letter. So, from the letters Fechheimer wrote, of which there are nearly four hundred, mostly signed 'S.S. Fletcher', an anglicised form of his difficult name, an intimate glimpse is gained of his life in the College. From these letters it becomes clear that nothing escaped O.B.'s eye and that no problem, however trivial, was too small to avoid his attention. The work, of course, was clearly defined by the Board of Education authorities, the College staff had only to arrange it – to compose the students' daily timetables and then, at the end of every week, to write O.B. a brief report. All this was comparatively simple although the report was often a struggle – on some occasions the 'last straw' in what was always a heavy programme. What was much more difficult, however, was the ordinary domestic administration. In these matters O.B.'s flair for tireless, detailed interference found a new authority and scope. Never since his time at Eton had he had so great an opportunity to order everybody else's business. He drove Fletcher nearly demented. At the end of 1904, for example, he accused him of ordering some household items which he, O.B., had never authorised. Fletcher became extremely upset. 'Dear Principal', the latter wrote,[5]

> Your letter has hurt me very much. It produces that very worry which interferes with good work, and of which you complain so much. It implies extravagance on my part, a charge which I feel undeserved, especially as I have saved the College expenditure which would more than cover the bill which is the occasion for your reproach. I have been very careful during the entire year not to order anything, but to do everything through you. Why then write: 'It shows me how important it is to keep these things in my hands.'?

O.B. as usual was unrepentant, and went on merrily as before. In February he tried to ration the coal. Fletcher wrote again, unhappily,

> I really wish I knew what has been the cause of our altered relationship during the last year. For more than five years we

worked in perfect harmony and without friction. You appeared to have confidence in me and as a result the work proceeded smoothly. For more than a year things seem to have altered entirely. You will not listen to anything I may have to say; you overrule me on every point and you seem to have withdrawn your confidence in me from me. I cannot understand why this should be so. I have been loyal to you, I have worked as hard if not harder than in previous years, and, I believe, with no diminution of power. But nothing I have done lately seems to meet with your approval. Work under such conditions becomes heartbreaking.

O.B. softened after this and told Fletcher with sudden intimacy of his hopes of becoming the Provost of King's. The incumbent, Austen Leigh, had died and O.B. seriously hoped to succeed him. Fletcher wrote that he was 'deeply touched' to be taken into O.B.'s confidence. When the appointment went to M.R. James – in fact, O.B. was never considered – Fletcher did his best to console him. O.B. gave him a set of cruets with a handsome stand in which to place them. Time passed, resentment with it; the former working harmony returned, and Fletcher signed his personal letters 'ever yours affectionately'.

As well as getting on with the staff, drawing from them their very best in spite of conflicts from time to time, O.B. managed to do the same with nearly all of his students. Love and affection in the best sense, admiration and profound gratitude, were expressed over and over again in the students' letters in these days. The number he received in fifteen years, until he retired at the age of seventy, many hundreds every year, filled his lonely heart with happiness. All the joy he had known at Eton, the warmth of the pupil-teacher relationship based on mutual need and respect, and without the interference of parents or the disapproval of higher authority, at last was granted him at Cambridge. Every day as he went to the College, tricycling over Parker's Piece and stumping into Warkworth House, he increased the love his students felt for him. He tutored every one of them himself, and knew every one of them intimately. Mostly boys from a humble class, mostly far away from home and from their parents for the first time, they found in him a father substitute. He, for his part, found in them the loving children he had never known. Unafraid and unchallenged, he beamed, a sun in a cloudless sky. Over and over again students tried to express their thanks for help given and kindness done, and found it almost impossible to do so.

On Monday I was so overwhelmed by your great sympathy & kindness that I could not adequately express my deep gratitude to you, & even now I am at a loss to find words efficient for my purpose. Your kind, father-like sympathy, so freely given, so deeply moved me that my thoughts turned to the oft quoted words
the elements
so mixed up in him that Nature might up
and say to all the world 'This was a man'[6]

So wrote Harry Dockerill after an unrecorded kindness.[7] These lines were often quoted by students trying to express their feelings. O.B.'s love had a universality which somehow spoke to them all.

One student in particular wrote O.B. a number of letters which deserve to be quoted at greater length because of the light they throw on O.B.'s influence. J.R. Jones came to the College in 1904. The son of a miner from Felin-Foel, a small village north of Llanelli, he won a Queen's Scholarship to Cambridge only to find, when it came to the point, that his family could not support the expense. He had to send O.B. a telegram saying he could not afford to come. Thereupon, O.B. himself, offered to give him £30, the missing portion of the annual sum required. When Jones's parents heard this they were quite unable to express their thanks. Their eldest son wrote for them – they probably only spoke Welsh, and most likely were also illiterate.[8]

Dear Sir. We are overwhelmed with gratitude. That is what I wrote in the telegram and I can think of no other sentence which can so nearly express our present feelings, which however, are too deep for words.

When my brother's telegram announcing your generous gift reached my parents, I was at a science lecture in Swansea. I did not reach home until very late, but it was quite early enough to find both my parents awaiting my arrival, telegram in hand and tears of joy in their eyes. We are truly grateful.

Could we, by our utmost exertions and privations have been able to maintain my brother, that sad telegram of yesterday morning would never have been dispatched. I fondly thought we would be able, but when my father came from the works and explained our circumstances, I saw that it was, as he said, quite impossible. And here I may say that father, who is a village Hampden, spends willingly every penny he can earn on his children's education. He has many and many a time worked extra hours to procure books for us.

We can certainly find £15 a year and perhaps £20. In fact we should be quite able to find £20 when I get a rise of £10 a year shortly.

I am quite at a loss for words to express our gratitude, but hope to show it by doing our very utmost for my brother. He and ourselves must, when we are able to, do unto others as you have so nobly done by us.

Jones's career at the D.T.C. was not as brilliant as his parents hoped, but he got his degree in 1907 as well as his Education Certificate. He himself came to admit he was not so bright as most of his friends, but what he lacked in academic flair he tried to make up by steady plodding. His report in the College 'Record of Students' shows that he worked extremely hard but lacked the magic touch of the teacher, the understanding of tender minds. In one class on which he was judged, teaching 'Things porous and soluble', he bored the boys to such an extent that they very nearly ran out of the building. The report notes that he 'lost his temper'. He was 'very Welsh', and 'Talked too much', and his 'Stimulating Power' was 'not much'. However, before he left the College, he had 'made some improvement'.

During these three years he wrote frequently to O.B. 'It is with unbounden love that my brother Will and the rest of the family thank you for your constant care of me', he told him at Christmas, 1905. 'Venerable Principal', he said in another letter,

The paedagogue seeks the Holy Grail

It is always said in Cambridge that a very great deal of the greatness of Mr. Browning is due to the fact that he always helps a person when a person is 'down' . . . When a man is 'down' most men forsake him and avoid him whereas you have a grand reputation for helping everyone in need of sympathy. True greatness consists of being able to go down to sympathise with weaklings like myself . . .

I made a resolution on reading your last letter, to work harder this vacation than I have ever done in my life. I sincerely thank you Mr. Browning for your kind words from time to time. Men like Bonner, Byron Scott and I will carry the name of Mr. Oscar Browning down to posterity as the name of a dear father. I do not think any man in England has a greater number of true friends than you, Mr. Browning. As Bonner aptly put it, 'The O.B. *knows* me; these others are *acquainted* with me'.

When my parents and I think of all you have done in our behalf, Mr. Browning, we fail to find words to express our thanks to you.

Jones left Cambridge in the summer of 1907 having taken a degree in Moral Science and Physics, and obtained his teacher's diploma. He went to Park Walk Boys' School, Chelsea, an important school with eight other masters and several hundred pupils. His annual salary was £110. From there he continued to write.

As one who hears occasionally from the ex-third-year students, I can assure you that they all agree that you are the best MAN they met while at Cambridge. You never forgot, what so few Cambridge dons bear in mind, that most of our Day Training College students leave home for the first time to enter their college course. The temptation to ape many of the richer undergraduates is great and personally I think you could do a great deal in showing how utterly impossible it is for the majority of us to copy the richer students in everything and how glaringly incongruous it is for a man to copy them in some things and not in others.

The paedagogue seeks the Holy Grail

You have directed the lives of so many hundreds of under-graduates that you perhaps are getting tired of their thanking you. Each individual undergraduate, whom you have from time to time taken in hand as you took me, feels after he leaves Cambridge that he owes more to you than any other man in the world. I attribute your success in directing young men to your acknowledgement of the fact that there is no stereotyped young man – that different people require different treatments.

Last summer Gibbon, Nicholas and I had a brief reunion at Mumbles of which reunion I daresay Nicholas has informed you. We three met for the first time at Cambridge and naturally our talk centred round the old place. I am sure you would have laughed heartily had you overheard us from behind one of those cliffs peculiar to Mumbles. Like three learned doctors we thought that we were quite qualified to compare the dons we had met at Cambridge. Though the O.B. did not come out unscathed from the ordeal, yet we three agreed that the O.B. was the best friend we had ever made. He certainly deserved the appellation of 'man'. We fully appreciated the fact that, though you were born a gentleman and had the best education that England could offer you in your earlier days, you never tried to damp that spring of sympathy which a man in affluence naturally has for a man in adversity. How many are those parvenus who inhibit this natural spring of sympathy in order to appear aristocratic! A great part of your success as Principal of the Day Training College is undoubtedly due to the paternal sympathy you extended to the students individually.

I must close with those well-chosen words of your friend Francis Money-Coutts which seem to ring in my ears whenever I see, read or think of you:

> And oh! how many, with more voice than I
> Can boast of eloquence, could tell the tale
> Of all they owe to you, of aims set high,
> Good purpose strengthened, thoughts that never fail
> To animate the spirit, till it fly
> Far over the sea and land to seek The Grail.[9]

CHAPTER XIII

Dropping the pilot

O.B. advanced in age and began to approach his allotted span. As the old century bowed to the new, and as many people at Cambridge and King's began to think he ought to retire, one last and supreme triumph was by the Gods awarded him. In the summer of 1898, it came about that an old pupil received the glittering appointment of Viceroy of India.

This, in itself, was nothing of note. Former pupils from Eton and King's served in every corner of the Empire in every rank from governor to general; and over a period of forty years in which the education of statesmen had been the avowed object of his life, he had seen his efforts frequently rewarded. In this particular case, however, his heart leapt when he heard the news: the new Viceroy was George Nathaniel Curzon.

Other hearts leapt, too, when they heard of George Curzon's appointment. In every Old Etonian group in every Indian regiment and club in every corner of the sub-continent, breasts filled with hope. Old Etonian links were strong. Every boy from O.B.'s house hoped that his would be even stronger. Curzon was actually known to have said in the august gardens of Marlborough House that he owed his very success to O.B. Every pupil felt convinced that one note of recommendation, one word in the Viceroy's ear, would ensure the fulfilment of all his dreams.

So quite suddenly O.B. had shoals of letters from his old pupils. They all asked the same favour. Could he possibly, by any chance, should he happen to dine with Curzon, drop an appropriate hint in the viceregal ear. In one case in which he did so, he also achieved a magical cure.

'How splendid of you to write to the Viceroy on my behalf,' an old King's pupil, Emile Secondé wrote from Lucknow in a letter bubbling with gratitude.[1]

How can I thank you sufficiently. Fancy my surprise on returning from ten days' leave in Calcutta where I received a royal 'Welcome Home!!' to find a packet awaiting me from Col. Dunlop Smith, Private Sec y to His Excellency informing me that the Viceroy had received a letter from you recommending me for employment in the Political Department, the rules on the subject being enclosed. I could scarcely contain myself for joy, 'car il me semblait qu j'avais deja un pied dans l'etrier.' When the news reached The Pater I am told that his attack of Gout vanished instantaneously. It is, indeed difficult to say which of us is the happier – through your extreme kindness.

Others, of course, were not so lucky. An old pupil, Charles Buckland, had been in India for twenty years. O.B. put in a word for him but he waited in vain for any result. 'My dear Browning,' he wrote from Calcutta, even before Lord Curzon had arrived,[2]

> You will be surprised to hear from me but I do not think you will mind my writing to ask you kindly, if you see Curzon, as you very probably will before he starts, to mention me to him and to say anything you feel justified in saying on my behalf. He will then doubtless be quite different to what he would otherwise. I have never met him . . . Was he your pupil? An Eton man in Calcutta was saying the other day that Curzon owes everything to you (as many of us owe much) as you had 'made him', 'brought him out', 'taught him', etc, so that it must be gratifying to you to see the success he has attained in public life. If he is disposed to be loyal to you & to Eton (& Balliol) he can easily do something good for me: e.g. there will be a vacancy in the Foreign Secyship very soon; and probably the Chief Commissioner of Assam will have to go home for his health in the spring . . . Curzon would do well to bring in a little fresh blood & show himself more independent than Elgin has been; the latter has left the patronage in the hands of his 'admirers'. I am just now rather on a shelf & may remain there to the end.

O.B. wrote; Curzon replied; and Buckland sent him 'a 1000 thanks'; but the years passed and nothing happened. 'Curzon knows me & is very civil, but does not do what he should for me!' Buckland told O.B. gloomily. Buckland stayed on the shelf, gathering dust, until he retired to South Kensington. Many people in O.B.'s life to whom he had shown habitual kindness, on reaching places of power and influence, found it quite convenient to forget him. To tell the truth, in middle-age, he became a bore and a social embarrassment. He talked incessantly about himself, and very often behaved outrageously. Curzon, however, repaid the debt if, indeed, there was one to pay, without a moment's hesitation. He asked O.B. to come and visit him, just as soon as he arrived in India. O.B. did so in 1902. Every single moment of the trip, from the day Buckland met him at Calcutta to the day he said goodbye to his bearer was, as he said in his *Memories*, 'a pure joy'.

To stay with the Empire's first delegate, the very shadow of the King himself, to whom every man bowed and every woman paid her curtsey; to be swept about in a government train; to be met at stations by high officials; to spend the day with Maharajahs; to be asked his commands by A.D.C.s, dressed superbly in shining uniforms; these delights and a thousand others were to him a taste of paradise.

There was a deeper happiness: that of being seen to be right, being publicly acknowledged and having one's action justified. The rejected seer, the prophet of George Curzon's brilliance, was proved to be wise before the multitude. Perhaps for the only time in his life, for the five weeks he stayed in India, he felt content and perfectly secure. At Government House he was Curzon's friend. As he took the air in the Viceroy's carriage he felt like someone he never was, a normal and whole person.

Such euphoria could not last. To ease the pain of leaving India and of saying goodbye to his many friends, not the least his Christian bearer whom he described as beautiful and black, he had planned to spend a week in Italy. While abroad he had kept in touch with a handsome Venetian boy called Norbut who had thanked him for his 'dear letters' and signed himself 'your little friend'. Actually, Norbut was nineteen. They had met the previous year at Marienbad, and exchanged photographs and tender promises. Norbut had offered to show him Venice, a city

O.B. knew well from previous visits with gondolieri. At the last moment, Norbut fell ill, and had to submit to an operation. O.B. spent his days alone, an extremely uncongenial activity. Thus the holiday came to an end. Many sorrows and disappointments now awaited him at Cambridge. The first, and shamefully public, of these, took place at the Cambridge Union. He had been the Treasurer for twenty-one years, and when he had left to visit Curzon, the first time in as many Lents that he had been unable to fulfil his duties, he had blandly supposed that when he came back he would once again return to his office. Like many another dictator, however, he found the truth of the old adage that the mice will play when the cat is away.

For several years, the committee had found him increasingly difficult. At meetings he spoke at tedious length; he had no knowledge of finance at all; to argue with him was quite impossible. He refused to listen to anybody else, and took offence if contradicted. Once he was safely out of the country, a plot was laid to have him replaced. When he came back for the summer term and tricycled over to the Union building just behind the Round Church, full of delight at his safe return and full of stories of his visit to Curzon, he found instead of a welcome home, only talk of plans for his resignation.

The news was given to the world at large in a double-page cartoon in the 'Special May Week Number' of *The Granta*. O.B. was shown as Bismarck, after the drawing by Sir John Tenniel, in which the ageing 'Iron Chancellor' was seen leaving the ship of state, descending the gangway to a waiting dinghy, watched from above by the German Emperor. The caricature was brilliantly done, and O.B. thoroughly enjoyed it; but his self-esteem was severely mauled.

His friends consoled him as best they could. They raised a testimonial subscription, and commissioned the artist, Lowes Dickinson, an old friend of O.B.'s and father of the philosophical writer, to paint a presentation portrait. A careful study of head and shoulders, it still hangs in the Union building.

Towards the end of the Michaelmas term they gave O.B. a farewell dinner. The menu is still preserved in the Minute Book, neatly tied with green ribbon, for November 8th 1902. There were ten courses with appropriate toasts, and O.B., now a guest for the first time for two decades, rose to speak when his turn was called.

His eyes glistened and his chin trembled as he thanked his hosts with real emotion for the pleasure and privilege of having served them. Many listened with emotion, too, aware in spite of their inevitable youth and their necessarily brief acquaintance that, as the Kaiser had done with Bismarck, they were closing the door on an epoch. They were doing something that had to be done, and taking part in a painful ceremony. As the cartoon's caption had it in bold letters below the drawing, they, the kaisers of the Cambridge Union, at last were 'Dropping the Pilot'.

Another painful disappointment which O.B. had to endure on his return to Cambridge from India was brought about by his colleagues. Every year at the end of November an election was held for the College Council, the executive body of King's College; and every year, as a matter of course, for more years than most could remember, one of its members had been O.B. He had not stood in 1901 because of his proposed absence abroad, but on his return he had taken it for granted that once more he would be elected. When the day came, however, he did not receive sufficient votes. Behind the scenes it had been agreed by sincere friends and enemies alike that the time had come, for better or worse, to give his place at last to another colleague.

For the truth was that for many years on this committee and many others he had made any serious discussion almost completely impossible. He had plagued the chair with points of order, argued about the smallest detail, and always treated any view which did not exactly accord with his own as a veiled threat or snub or insult. No one could make him understand that such behaviour was difficult or wrong; and even those who had known him longest who, in a way were his oldest friends, could not make him behave like a normal person.

In those days before the telephone, whenever a meeting had

broken up, letters asking for explanations or demanding out-
right, abject apologies from all those who had dared oppose him
flew from one staircase to another, across the shadowy college
courts, like whirling leaves in a winter storm. The files concerning King's are crammed with them. From the Bursar, alone,
there are three hundred. The latter, W.H. Macaulay, tried
putting the matter simply with regard to another College body
from which O.B. had been excluded. Why had O.B. not been
appointed? Might he, Macaulay, explain the reason? 'This
reason is that discussion with you on any subject about which
you hold a strong view is often unsatisfactory, and sometimes
impossible.'

He received a third and shattering rebuff from Cambridge
University itself. As every author in the world knows, writing
books is considered a hobby; and only superb reviews and sales,
the outward and visible signs of success, will convince friends
and enemies alike that writing has any point or merit. In the
purer ranks of academic life where one slim volume alone may
take the author twenty years, and sales and reviews are often
minimal, only the grant of a Litt.D. will persuade colleagues
and other academics that precious time has not been wasted.

O.B. in this respect, had always fallen between two stools.
His popular works were not very good, with the possible excep-
tion of his *George Eliot* and perhaps, also, his *Flight to Varennes*.
Thirty years of planning and research had not produced his
magnum opus.

Nevertheless, in 1903, with more than twenty books behind
him, many of which were historical studies, and innumerable
pamphlets and printed lectures, he felt that the time had come
to apply for a Doctorate.

Having sounded out his friends and consulted the various
appropriate authorities, he got together copies of his books and
sent them in with a suitable letter to the Special Board for
History and Archaeology. This was the sub-committee of the
Senate which, in his particular case, recommended degrees for
English Literature.

In the following February, 1904, he heard from the Chairman,

Dropping the pilot

J.S. Reid, one of the leading historians in Cambridge, that his application had not been granted. Stung almost as never before, certainly not since Hornby had sacked him, he sent the Chairman a bitter protest. 'My dear Reid', he wrote from King's,[3]

> I have now received all the books I sent you including the 'Colleoni' which was returned by another hand. I observe that the leaves of 'The Flight to Varennes' have not been cut. I am surprised that volumes containing so much sound historical research should have been thought unworthy of an honour which was accorded to so inferior a production as Rose's Napoleon. Also it appears to me a scandal that a person of my age and standing who has done so much work for the University should not have an opportunity of separating himself from the mass of Masters of Arts, and of taking part in public functions with dignity and comfort. In no other University in the world would such service have been denied so meagre a recognition. So far as my information extends the Degree Committee have I think committed a serious error, and it is some comfort to me that I have reason to believe that this view is shared by those of its members whose opinion is, in my judgement, most entitled to respect.
>
> Believe me, Yrs sincerely, Oscar Browning.

Reid, of course, declined to reply except to explain that *The Flight to Varennes* had not been cut for a sensible reason: the Committee members had read it already.

The underlying truth was painfully clear to the whole of Cambridge. The coveted degree of Doctor in Letters was not given for historical journalism, nor for so-called research in the field; least of all for an expedition, however well and vividly described, made by a don on tour in France on a tricycle. O.B., however much he loved history, however much he knew and wrote, was not really in the proper sense, a serious professional historian. As head of the King's School of History he had brought the standard up to a level of which he had every right to be proud; but this was due to his gift for teaching. He knew all his students personally; coached them himself in his own rooms; made them join his Political Society; and however little he

actually taught, he inspired them to study and analyse the past
with delight as well as scholarly passion in a way they had never
done before.

The result was all that he might have expected. History
became a popular subject, and quite soon it was being read by a
third of all the students at King's. Yet, his success went
unrewarded; and when he was dropped from the College
Council to which, as head of the School of History, he had every
right to expect to belong, he felt an extreme pang of bitterness.
Never ready to suffer in silence, he wrote a long letter to W.H.
Macaulay which ended up with a stinging reproach. 'Twenty-
nine years of labour in this place have made me familiar with
the fact, that, in my case at least, any success which I may
obtain is met, not by reward as recognition, but by the inven-
tion of some new form of insult. I expected something better
than this from your tenure of the Tutorship and I much regret
that I am disappointed.'[4]

He sent a circular round to the Fellows.[5]

There are at the present moment thirty-nine Historical students in
King's College. History is the most numerous and in some respects
the most distinguished study in the College. It has in recent years
contributed more Fellows to the foundation than any other study.
It is the only study in which King's is preeminent above other
Colleges in its University Honours. Since the foundation of the
Historical Tripos in 1875 King's has obtained forty-one first
classes, whereas no other College has obtained more than twenty-
five. King's is well known outside its own walls as *par excellence* the
Historical College of Cambridge. History is a study of which the
College ought to be proud and which it ought to do its best to
foster. Yet at the present moment there is not a single Historical
student at King's who holds a foundation scholarship.

The reason for this was easy to explain. There were excellent
scholars among the students, but O.B.'s widespread reputation
as a hack historian and mere journalist necessarily over-
shadowed them. It was not felt that while he was there too much
money ought to be spent. For amongst other considerations,

Dropping the pilot

O.B. marked their papers himself. Very often, so it was said, he gave better marks to men who expressed views close to his own, than to others who tried to prove their worth with work showing original thought and research. Thus the College stayed its hand. After meetings of the College Council, talks were held by the Provost and Fellows, not on granting foundation scholarships, but how on earth, without a fuss, O.B. could be made to retire.

In these vintage years at King's, the first decade of the twentieth century, the years of Lowes Dickinson and Forster, of Maynard Keynes and Rupert Brooke, many people who came to the College left their impressions of O.B. He was good, bad, a fool, a genius; every adjective seemed to fit him. No one saw him better, however, than a man who had lately come back to Cambridge, his old acquaintance, Arthur Benson, who had just been elected a Fellow of Magdalene. Benson kept a private diary in which with the pen of a trained observer, and the spirit of a fellow patron of youth, he drew a picture of O.B. on which Boswell himself could not have improved. Benson had known O.B. for years – since he himself had been at Eton and King's – and had kept in touch with him ever since. In his periodical letters he had always written in a friendly manner. Now at Cambridge he saw him frequently. The spirit of friendship still remained; but in his diary he recorded, too, many paragraphs about O.B. which were barbed with unmalicious but deadly criticism.

On February 5th 1904, Benson dined with O.B.[6]

I got there at 8.0 . . . a *very* good little dinner, all cooked in his gyp room, at a gas stove! Soup, fish, a turkey, apple tart, and with it a really magnificent bottle of Schloss Johannesburg Hoch. O.B. tells me he has sixty kinds of wine in his cellar!

All this served by a young, sleepy-looking handsome sort of boy, apparently much depressed . . . Letters came in in the middle, which O.B. opened & read with avidity, & laughed a loud forced laugh over one. Then he fell into long tangled broken sentences, like a thorn thicket – some of which never came to an end, & some conducted from heaven knows where. Mostly about the infamous character of all Public Schools. Then he suddenly began to tell me about the letter which made him laugh. A strange story. It seems that he lately applied for a Litt. D. degree, thro' Ward of Peterhouse, who wrote cordially. He sent several books to the Degree Committee – & two days ago they sate, and *refused the application.* I honestly think this is a scandal . . . But the sad point was to find O.B. taking it all the wrong way. Putting it down to jealousy & scheming, & never for a *moment* considering whether *he* might be in any way to blame. He said one very characteristic thing at this point – the flow of talk had been *continuous* – when he suddenly said 'Of course it's jealousy mainly *as you say.*' Now I had not said a word. He read me out all the letters & documents, & almost covered me, where I sate, with a heap of his rejected books, like the robin & the Children in the wood.

My heart bled for the poor little man, who really has some genius, & who is laborious, kindly, public-spirited & devoted; but spoils it all by this transcendent egotism, by incessant *claims* for admiration etc. He kept on walking or rather trundling about the room in his absurd dress jacket, smoking, losing his cigar, finding papers, reading extracts – laughing uneasily etc. On we went . . . and then suddenly came rather a noble vein 'Well', he cried 'I have given my heart to King's, & my life & energies to the work of the College – & it fulfils all my dearest hopes; it is full of keen, enthusiastic young men, and growing daily before one's eyes – one can well afford to sink one's own personal disappointments in the happiness of that!'

It is very pathetic & makes me unhappy to see this man who is a man with a real touch of genius, full of enthusiasm, interest, aspiration, laborious, affectionate, hopeful, energetic, *wallowing* in this dreadful slough of self. I can't help feeling him to be a great man, somehow; & he has done an enormous amount of unrecognised work for the College. But if he has not received the recognition of others for it, he has received full measure, pressed down and running over, *from himself.* That is it. He never fails to remind everyone of what he has done, and to grasp the credit for a good deal that he has not done. There is something very sad at the thought of how *nearly* he is a really great man; & something ironical in the working of Providence wh. can allow it all to be spoilt at the last moment, so to speak, & turned rancid. *Sunt lacrimae rerum!*

Dropping the pilot

If O.B. was a sad failure, at least in the eyes of Arthur Benson and many others of the same age, he still held an august charm for the young men who came to King's and who continued to flock to his Sunday receptions.

His principal admirer at this time, his last at Cambridge as it proved, was a boy called Michaelides. He arrived as an undergraduate in Michaelmas, 1901, and at once found in O.B., under whom he was reading History, a fatherly quality of understanding to which his personality responded. To O.B., the affair was delightful. He was just setting off to India; and, for a moment forgetting his *rendezvous* with Norbut, the 'little friend' he had met in Marienbad, he tried to persuade Michaelides to come to the same city to join him. This could not be arranged, however. At least on the long voyage out, he was able to write affectionate letters, sure by then of his real attachment. He wrote, too, to the boy's mother. She, like her son, responded fervently.

At King's, as in every small and closed society, everyone noticed each other's foibles and gossiped cheerfully about their discoveries. O.B.'s love for Michaelides was soon the funniest joke of the term. Nathaniel Wedd, one of his colleagues, a man who had always liked O.B., wrote about it in his private journal, now safely in the College Library.

Sometimes certainly O.B.'s power of idealisation did lead to ridiculous results. This was notably the case with a certain Constantine Michaelides, the son of an American lady and a Liverpool Greek. The lad came to King's with a history scholarship from Crosby School, Liverpool. He had a wonderful gift of phrase-making and a certain intellectual audacity that completely captivated O.B. One of O.B.'s favourite remarks to scholars who thought well of themselves was; 'Well, you seem an awful swell in your own eyes. You are a swell, I know. But I tell you this: in your old age you will have only one source of pride, one thing to boast of. You will talk of the days "When I was at King's with Michaelides" ' This remark, often made in the presence of the hero himself, seemed to many people injudicious.

173

Dropping the pilot

In spite of Wedd's critical judgement, the Michaelides story ended happily. He took a first class degree; and although he did not become an historian, he employed his manifest talents and charm in the diplomatic service.

O.B.'s time was drawing to a close. Both at King's in the School of History, and in the Teachers' Training Syndicate, plans had been made to make him retire. Once again, to quote from Benson for the year 1905:

> A long letter from O.B., & a very sad one. He is 68, & in order to get rid of him the College are going to pass a superannuation rule, superannuating at 70. He writes such a letter; and incloses a still worse one to the Provost, in which he says plainly that he thinks the whole prosperity & success of the History School at King's are due to him & depend on him, & he thinks it to the interest of King's to keep him there till he drops.
>
> I wrote a long letter back of 20 sides, urging him in the name of dignity, to choose a successor, train him, and then retire himself and write.
>
> He says that it would be 'a sentence of death' to him, that he could not with any dignity continue to live at Cambridge etc., etc. All this is very pathetic; & what makes it more so is that there is not one single person who wants him to stay, or wd be sorry if he died.
>
> It is an awful picture – So greedy, vain, foul-minded, grasping, ugly, sensual a man on the one hand; & on the other, the traces of an old glory about him, like faded and tarnished gilding. A youth, a spring, an energy, a love of beauty – so sweet in themselves, yet harbouring so ill in this gross & tun-like frame.

When the day came to retire, and no honours came his way – no Fellowships of other colleges, no memberships of Learned Societies, no honorary degrees or doctorates – O.B. behaved with unexpected dignity, made plans to vacate his rooms, and retire to a house he had bought in Sussex.

Suddenly the thought of King's College without O.B.'s absurd figure billowing out of College Chapel, waddling across the sacred lawns, tumbling onto his grotesque tricycle, or puffing up the stairs to his rooms, was beyond the ordinary imagination. The School of History gave him a dinner, and so,

174

too, did the Political Society; each one with appropriate speeches, and sumptuous *entrées* like 'Soles a l'O.B.', and sweets like 'Gateaux Historiques'. His old opponent, Austen Chamberlain, by that time a famous man, the Worcestershire contest long forgotten, proposed the toast of 'Our Guest'. Benson wrote a graceful ode which was published in the *Cambridge Review*.

Many, many people wrote to him, not a few who had never met him, who knew only his reputation as the student's guide and counsellor and friend. Of these, one was Henry Moxon, an undergraduate of St John's College, whose letter contains the spirit of them all.[7]

April 1909

Dear Sir

Though I have not the pleasure of knowing you personally I *very* greatly admire the kind and homely way you treat the students. In an age like today when most college 'Dons' are usually very musty, and live out of the world, you are a splendid example of kindliness. Your social evenings with coffee, music and 'smiles' are first rate. Yet Cambridge masters live in an atmosphere of Greek, Hebrew and bigotry in most cases. You don't.

Yours very truly, Henry Moxon

In placid retirement at Bexhill where he had bought a house next to his sister Mariana, who had moved there in 1900 with her school, he began to write his *Memories of Sixty Years*. The pure air and gleaming sea revived his spirits and sexual reveries, and he wrote a dedicatory verse to the Vice Provost of Eton College in characteristically doubtful taste, of which he sent the latter a draft.

To F.W. Cornish

Vice Provost of Eton College

In youth we roamed, a merry band,
Through mead and desert, hand in hand,
With Dick and Henry, Charles and George,
The fetters of our life to forge,
We strove and quarrelled, fought and kissed,
And not a fount of joy was missed.

175

'I forbid "kissed" ', Cornish wrote when he returned the draft. ' "Kissed" suggests an entirely unknown relation.'

Needless to say, O.B. paid no attention to him, and he published the poem unaltered. After all, 'kissed' rhymed with 'missed', and that was really the point of using it. If anyone chose to misunderstand, there was nothing that he, O.B., could do to prevent them. Furthermore, no less a person than Sir George Otto Trevelyan, the great Macaulay's nephew, a very distinguished man in his own right, wrote to tell him how much he had liked the book, especially the '16 lines to Cornish which . . . delighted me singularly'.

So O.B. felt quite satisfied. The book was well received, too, by the general public. The reviews were good, except in *The Times*. It was, in fact, probably O.B.'s best book, for this kind of historical survey about himself suited his narrative manner perfectly. In the general flow of interest there was no need for accuracy. A kiss here or there, sixty years previously with the Vice Provost of Eton was really quite irrelevant.

In these years before the Great War, he wrote and travelled extensively. Mariana died in 1910, and from that time he felt free to wander wherever he liked. His fame and extraordinary appearance were such that people recognised him everywhere; and he always carried gilt-edged visiting cards and a packet of photographs in his pocket to give to his admirers. A Mrs Nuttall who had met him on a Lunn's Tour of the Middle East on which he had given some lectures wrote for a photograph, afterwards, recollecting his 'genial, kindly, gently dignified personality'. An old cousin, Augusta Ann Oliver, told him that even a shop-girl had known who he was when she took his photograph into a store for a frame.

On this Lunn's Tour he had made his last, passionate conquest: a boy called Msabbek, his dragoman in Jerusalem. The boy was aged sixteen. O.B., always finding perfection in youth, described him as having a 'face like a young Christ'. Many interesting hours were passed between them. When they parted, both were upset. 'My Dearly beloved friend & father Oscar Browning,' Msabbek wrote later. 'How are you getting

on now with your work & who do look after you & put on your
evening dress & soccs & brush you close & put them in order &
who do walk with you about when you want some besness. How
are you getting on with your Arabic. I hope you are getting on
well.'⁸ O.B. sent him a jersey, and Msabbek sent O.B. some olive
oil soap.

Reading and writing letters took up a great part of O.B.'s
time for the rest of his life. People wrote to him from all over the
world. One of his prize possessions was a postcard from Japan
addressed simply to 'The O.B., Cambridge'. As is the lot of all
prominent figures, he had many letters from cranks and luna-
tics. A window cleaner in Liverpool told him that he was being
hypnotised and made to perform 'acts of moral depravity'
against his will. He pleaded for O.B.'s help. Miriam Ellis asked
O.B. to take a note of the shape of the ears of the choristers in
King's College Chapel. Gertrude Stuart sent him a copy of, 'For
he's a jolly good fellow' in Esperanto, a language in which he
took an interest. A.H. Clarke wrote from Brixton to tell him that
there was a prophecy 'of the most direct kind' to one of O.B.'s
ancestors in Gibbon. T. Todd Potts told him that he had
dreamt that O.B. would be 'God's ambassador on earth for
Napoleon' and so win for his soul at last 'a crown greater than
all the crowns of Europe'.

It was quite easy for O.B. to believe this last prophecy, for the
older he got, the more the Emperor's tragedy haunted him. He
admired the First Consul more than any other historical figure.
Years of study of his life had made him so familiar with it that, in
his more psychic moments, he half believed that he did carry
Napoleon's spirit within him. At Bexhill, he called his house
'Tilsit' after the Prussian town in which Napoleon met the
defeated Alexander I in 1807. He called his garden 'Longwood'
after the district of the same name at St Helena. Napoleon's
portrait hung in the dining room, decorated with a garland of
dried flowers which he, himself, had picked by the Emperor's
grave on the island. 'It will take another hundred years for
Englishmen to understand Napoleon', he said on one occasion
'the best man that ever lived in the world except Jesus Christ.'

Dropping the pilot

He travelled extensively in these years, giving lectures and attending conferences. Among other places, he went to Russia to give a series of talks on the 'Ideals of Education'. 'Your name is so well known in Russia', the President of St Petersburg Guild of English Teachers told him, 'that we are confident a course of lectures by you would prove a great success.' The President was right in his prediction. Nevertheless, when O.B. spoke unexpectedly to two retired English governesses, he caused them to suffer 'feelings of consternation'. Later, the misunderstanding was cleared up. He lunched with the British Ambassador, Sir Arthur Nicolson, and was the lion of the occasion.

When he was at home, he wrote for two or three hours every morning before breakfast – letters, histories, and poems in various languages. In Latin he composed an ode in Horatian Alcaics to The Penis.[9]

Unconscionable Love

> Partner of our days, king potent over men,
> troublesome author of anxieties, you are
> the fountain of pleasure, but also of
> innumerable pains . . .

He sent a copy to his old friend Frank Money-Coutts, who had become Lord Latymer. 'The meaning is very subtle', he told him, 'but I expect you will understand it. It is superficially rather smutty, but intrinsically very religious and spiritual. I think that it is very good, but then I always think my own writings good.' In Italian, French and English, he wrote of love.

> There's someone in this place I hold so dear
> I have to pray upon my knees at night
> He may not prove my idol before God
> Someone I love so well that I have said
> Scarce anything to anyone of him.

His versification was not very inspiring, but it relieved his feelings. Admirers, in their turn, indited poems to him. W.C.

Dropping the pilot

Clarke, of Hastings, sent him a sonnet, 'Composed and dedicated to Professor Oscar Browning after hearing him lecture on John Keats'.

> So when great minds will stoop to lend their aid
> How willingly our eager souls expand
> Responsive to the touch of that kind hand
> In which our own confidingly is laid!
> So would we render thanks that thou didst bring
> A grateful draft from the Pierian Spring.

O.B. hated being alone, and when he was by himself, his normal feelings of optimism and activity were overcast. Over and over again at these times, he went back in memory to the long-ago days at Eton when he had been dismissed; and to the most recent era at King's when he had been superannuated. It had not been fair. No one had understood him.

Then his eye would light on something, perhaps a book in the local library, and his spirits would bubble up. One day he found a copy of Pear's Encyclopaedia for one shilling, and started reading its 'Prominent People'. To his delight, he found he was amongst them. He was frightfully pleased with his discovery, and wrote to his old friend and colleague Nathaniel Wedd, who was still at King's, to tell him about it. The section, he explained, contained '. . . about 3000 names of all the most prominent people who had lived in all ages & countries since the creation of the world. I AM IN IT.'

He celebrated the event with an epigram. In a curious way, it recorded his life in a nutshell. His striking appearance, exuberant health, his chequered careers at Eton and King's, all reduced in a squib composed by himself to something faintly ridiculous.

> His name is O.B. he's a darling, a duck
> Looks remarkably young for his years
> Though at Eton and Cambridge they gave him the chuck
> He's a prominent person in Pears.

179

CHAPTER XIV

Oscar Browning, O.B.E.

O.B. was in Rome when the Great War broke out. The unhappy Malvina Wortham had died in 1911, only a year after Mariana. Her penniless husband, Biscoe, was still alive, but O.B. had no wish to see him. He had no one else to draw him back to England. So he decided to stay where he was in Italy.

There was another reason. His prostate gland had for many years been a source of pain and inconvenience to him, and, so he believed, the cause of libidinous thoughts. In 1912, when in Rome, it had been removed after a sudden emergency. He had never felt better in his life than after its removal, and he wished to remain near the doctors and surgeons who had looked after him. He had always told his doctor in Sussex that there was something wrong with it. Now he was able to prove he was right, as he loved doing more than anything else in the world. It had weighed two hundred and twenty grams! He sent it back to Dr Skryne in Bexhill in a bottle.

Furthermore, life was much cheaper in Italy than it was in England. With a pension from King's he had £700 a year, and was really quite comfortably off. He was able to live in the manner he liked and, in a quiet way, to continue to enjoy the status of a personality. All sorts of people came to see him; in fact, as at King's, if anyone visited the circle in which he moved, and failed to meet him, they felt cheated, and made an effort to obtain an introduction. So his social life was almost as busy as ever.

With all the time in the world to write letters, he communicated at length with all his old friends and colleagues, retired or otherwise, at Cambridge and elsewhere, and gave many cheerful and detailed accounts of the way his time was passing. 'My dear Wedd', he wrote from the Palazzo Simonetti on January 13th 1916,[1]

Oscar Browning, O.B.E.

Here I was never so happy in my life & perhaps never so well. I eat sleep digest admirably &, the doctor says, I have the arteries of a young man. I am very busy. I gave a course of lectures before Christmas and am to give another course beginning on Monday next my 79th birthday. On that day also a number of distinguished people, chiefly historians, give me a complimentary dinner – very embarrassing. I am not used to it. I am accustomed to kicks but not to halfpence. They never did it at King's except undergraduates. A day or two ago I typed at my desk sedens sedili in uno from 2.45 p.m. til 7.15 one of my lectures & felt all the better for it. Not bad for a man of my age. I have taken a lovely flat with a large terrace overlooking the Tiber, and a spacious bedroom behind, flooded with sunshine, absolutely quiet. I am looked after by three angels, one male, two female, ie: my Secretary Ettore Antinori, his mother and little sister aged 13. They will cherish me while I am well, treat me when I am ill, and bury me when I am dead. I enjoy the best society in Europe. Could I wish for anything better?

If there was anything it was the presence of royalty, sadly lacking in war-time Italy, but a short time before the armistice even this delight was granted him. In May 1918, the Prince of Wales paid an official visit to Rome, and O.B. received an invitation to the British Embassy to meet him. O.B.'s cup of happiness overflowed. He records in his *Memories of Later Years* how tears filled his eyes and a lump rose in his throat as he talked to him. As he had known the Prince's mother for many years, from the days when, as Duchess of York, she used to visit Cambridge, he decided to write and tell her what a great success the Prince's visit had been. She must have smiled when she received his letter, filled as it was with characteristically personal flatteries and compliments.[2]

Palazzo Simonetti
Via Pietro Cavallini
Roma

June 1st 1918

Mr. Oscar Browning presents his humble duty to your Majesty and hopes that your Majesty will pardon the liberty he takes in writing these lines. He cannot allow the visit of his Royal Highness the Prince of Wales to Rome to pass without recording the effect which it has produced on everyone, and the enthusiasm which it has excited amongst the inhabitants of Rome and the Italian Nation at large. The personal charm of His Royal Highness, his pure, simple, beautiful and manly countenance, his exquisite manners and his feminine sympathy for all with whom he has come into contact has caused an affectionate emotion which is unique in Mr. Browning's experience.

No Englishman could meet His Royal Highness without feeling proud of him, and being thankful that God has given him Parents who have been responsible for an education for which the whole Country must be thankful & proud.

O.B.'s literary work flourished, also, throughout this time. Before and during the war he published *A History of the Modern World, A General History of the World*, and *A Short History of Italy*; in all, more than two million words, the equivalent of, perhaps, sixteen ordinary novels. They were none of them very good and in terms of scholarship, they were useless; but at least they brought him in some useful money. He was more interesting when he wrote about writing them, as he did to many of his friends. Had he put these thoughts into his lectures at Cambridge, his reputation as an historian might have been higher; for they revealed, for better or worse, how he arrived at his many unorthodox judgements.

Writing to Charles Webster, a former pupil, and young Fellow of King's, he said,[3]

I am very glad that you have done so much research. I did a great deal when I was your age and found it most fascinating. But do not depend too much upon it. The real foundation of history is psychology, not original documents. Documents are always misleading and often false. Make up your mind about a man first, & then correct it by documents. You can never construct him out of documents.

I am enjoying myself here very much and working hard. I begin at 5, read my Bible according to the advice to Bryce, then drink my first cup of tea – my second at six – read what I have to read, dress at seven, write letters and begin typing my book. I am finishing my History of Mediaeval Italy which I began in 1878 and I write it straight off with the typewriter. [He was working on the 62nd chapter, of a planned total of 70.]

At twelve I go for an hour's walk till lunch at one. After lunch I read the papers carefully – very interesting just now, & then go into Society. I know all the most interesting people in Rome, and it is the most intellectual society in the world. I rarely have a dull moment.

He wrote also, at length and often to Goldie Lowes Dickinson, Fellow of King's, son of the artist, with whose family O.B. had enjoyed a friendship stretching back fifty years to his days as a master at Eton.[4]

I do not know whether it is because I am a Christian Scientist but I am a hopeless optimist about the war. I think that it will do good all round except perhaps in the U.S.A. which does not matter, where they will get disgustingly and perilously rich and will have lost all claim to be a high-minded nation, devoted to high ideals. To England it is a godsend, it is the only thing which could cure us from the cankering maladies which beset us for which there was no other remedy. Luckily it came before our malady discharged itself *internally* & stopped the ruin just before it burst fatally.

I was never so happy in my life as I am now, & never better in health. I look back on Eton & King's with something like horror, but I tried to do my best there. I was not made to be a College Don. I work hard . . . I am trying to write & *speak* Russian. I can read it & have a professor twice a week . . .

Goodbye, my dear Goldie, and sometimes in your prayers remember the cheerful and optimistic wretch who still loves you and all good people.

O.B.'s views on the war were more common amongst European intellectuals than is often remembered; at the beginning, at least, until the full horror and futility of modern combat had revealed itself. It was not Christian Science that gave O.B. his detached and uncritical opinion of the conflict, but simply the spirit of the circle in which he moved.

Oscar Browning, O.B.E.

Once the war was over he just forgot about it. So many people were now able to come and see him. There were former pupils, students, and lovers; a poet, Herbert Sleigh, who showered him with effusions of suffocating length and boredom; the famous, the rich, the curious; Biscoe's son, Hugo Wortham, who became his heir and biographer; and many other nephews and nieces of a younger generation. He was pleased to see them all, and never got tired of them.

He had only one small worry at this time – about the disposal of his body after he died. He wished to be cremated, and his ashes to be laid in the Chapel at King's. He wrote to the Vice Provost about it and obtained his agreement in principle. Then he approached the British Ambassador and asked if provisional arrangements might be made for his ashes to be taken back to England by Diplomatic Bag. 'Hilarious despatches' flew back and forwards between London and Rome on this difficult matter of international practice. Eventually it was settled, and O.B. was promised a dignified last journey, honoured by a special protocol.

In the last year of his life he received, at length, an honour from the British Government. It was not entirely unsolicited. He had long felt that some sort of recognition for his work ought to be given him. In a letter of 1919 to George Curzon he had asked him what could be done about it. 'Could you possibly get me made a KBE? I should ask for it on the grounds of propaganda, for which many have been decorated. I doubt if anyone, except perhaps George Trevelyan, has done more than I have to make English and Italians understand each other.'[5]

The idea of O.B. being made a Knight was a joke that no one except himself took seriously. When he did get given an honour, once again everyone laughed except O.B. himself. In the Birthday Honours List for 1923 he was created an Officer of the Order of the British Empire – in other words, he was made an OBE.

He received it formally at the British Embassy from the Chargé d'Affaires, and felt as pleased as a child with a new trinket. He wrote and thanked George Curzon for his part in the

184

matter. It was, he told him, 'a splendid ornament in admirable taste'.

He was now aged eighty-five and consciously failing. After all the millions of words he had penned over the years, 'writer's cramp' had deprived him of the use of his right hand. However, he used a typewriter. His life and habits and thoughts and pleasures were becoming increasingly simple. Yet, still, really, he remained in perfect health. Writing to E.M. Forster in May of this year he told him, 'I sleep well, eat no meat, drink no wine, live on fruit and eggs. This morning I ate four apples & six oranges, about my usual allowance. My only weakness is my legs, I always use a stick and generally a "bastone vivente".'

The following year he summed up his life's achievements in a letter to Professor Browne, Fellow of Pembroke College.

I am getting very old and am now 86 so that I sometimes think whether I have really done my duty in life. I worked very hard to make Eton a good place of education. I signally failed and got sacked for my pains. No one has taken up my work and athletics reign supreme. It no longer educates statesmen but has become an army school and contents itself with Generals. The Provost writes ghost stories and the Headmaster silly novels. At Cambridge I did better. I think that I really founded New King's and it has gone on splendidly since. I consider it now the best College at Cambridge, the most original, the most independent and the most vigorous. It has ceased to be a great historical college from the preponderating influence of Sheppard and Keynes but I believe that I had much to do with making History popular and the great success of the History School owes I think something to me. It certainly owes little or nothing to Acton although it is a great glory to have had him at Cambridge. For the training of teachers including the Training College I deserve all the credit, because I imagined and invented it and that is now very flourishing and, what is more, respected by the University. So I think I have done some work in my life.[6]

Music remained his greatest pleasure. Every Thursday he gave a musical party at which a quartet played works by Mozart and Haydn. Like Goethe, he felt Beethoven too power-

185

ful for him. His friends came, male and female. They said it was the best music in the city. His interest in languages, of which he had learnt or studied at least thirty-six, remained as strong as ever. He began lessons in Hebrew, wishing to read the Old Testament in the original tongue. At the same time, he was having his portrait painted by Emanuel Gliecenstein. 'It was truly moving', the painter said, as he sat with him, 'to see with what effort he recited the first line, the creation of the world, in Hebrew.'

He had no anxiety whatsoever about death. In spite of flirtations with the cult of Mary Baker Eddy, and with spiritualism, he remained a firm adherent of the Christian faith in which he had been brought up with its promise of redemption and everlasting life. So the idea of moving from one sphere to another held out absolutely no fear for him. Indeed, he looked forward to it. Would he not be united once again with his mother whom he had missed and prayed for and thought about every single day of his life since her death in 1888? Her photograph hung above his bed. He wrote about her.

> Whene'er at night I lie awake,
> Faces possession of me take,
> And clustering round from out the gloom,
> Beset me in my little room.
> Mother, with voice and manner mild,
> Keeps watch upon her darling child,
> And, loving both, in serious mood,
> Arrests the bad and stirs the good.

The end came on the 6th October. He had been ill for three weeks, following a slight stroke, and on that morning, with little promise of life left, his three 'angels', the Antinoris, were gathered at his bedside. Suddenly he asked that the little girl, Rosina, should leave the room. Then, lying back, holding the young Ettori's hand, he died quietly.

His ashes were, as he wished, taken back to England by Diplomatic Bag, and laid to rest at King's. Benson attended the ceremony and, as usual, recorded it in his diary; less charitably than in the past when, in spite of all, he had admired O.B. more than he had disliked him.

Wed. O.B.'s memorial service, sweetly sung unaccompanied. Provost absent. I sat next the Vice Chancellor, Mann conducted. Milner-White read beautifully & Macaulay the lesson very feebly – poor attendance. A very meaningless affair. O.B. had been out of mind for years, & he did fully as much harm as good at King's, & was latterly a great nuisance. What with fellowships & pensions he drew £700 a year from King's. I can't imagine that his death will cause any grief or create a sense of loss or make any difference to any human being.

There was one person to whom O.B.'s death was a real loss: his nephew Hugo, the son of Biscoe and Malvina Wortham. O.B. had always liked Hugo, and in the difficult days of Biscoe's arrest and financial chaos had taken pity on him. He had seen him through King's as an undergraduate, and had kept in close touch with him ever since. Hugo was musical and literary, understood O.B.'s foibles, and felt no criticism of them. He had promised to write O.B.'s biography. O.B. had made him his heir and literary executor.

So it fell to Hugo to go to Rome and settle O.B.'s estate which he did with genuine sorrow. There was very little to do, and very little of value in O.B.'s remaining possessions. O.B. had given many of his books to King's; had auctioned many others at Sotheby's; and had presented the rest, some three thousand volumes, to the Hastings Public Library. He had sold all his letters from Oscar Wilde, George Eliot, Tennyson, Swinburne, and many other famous people. He had donated to King's, the Cambridge Union, and to Eton the portraits of himself by Zuloaga, Lowes Dickinson, and Teague which had been painted in his later years. He had disposed of his house at Bexhill. In the process, because he had been so far away, he had lost many other smaller items of value and literary interest. In the end, there remained for Hugo only two drawings of O.B. by Simeon Solomon; a plaster medallion relief of O.B. by William

Story; a great many private papers, as many as one hundred thousand by Hugo's estimate; and some money.

Perhaps, in a way, the money was the most important. It was a kind of barometer. It might be said to indicate what the world had thought of O.B. after all these years of intense and restless effort, and of the things he himself had placed most value in – History and Paedagogy.

He had fifteen years at Eton, and thirty years at Cambridge, during which time he had seen many of his pupils rise to the heights of their professions, he had written books, articles, lectures, not to mention letters, to the extent of something like ten million words. Yet, in the course of all this, financial reward had escaped him, and his bank balance had never increased with his age or success or activities. A seedsman in Lincolnshire, Pennell by name, had once written him a telling letter. O.B. had made a complaint. Pennell had replied with ironic politeness, 'We regret to have your complaint about garden seeds, which we venture to think is a little unusual; you have indeed succeeded where others have failed and failed where others have succeeded.'

That was the simple truth about O.B.'s life. He had failed to be the man he ought to have been, the successful author, scholar and academic. He had succeeded in being what many others would like to have been, the acknowledged friend of youth and learning everywhere, a man whose kindness and eccentricity had become a legend in his own lifetime. The only trouble was that a man has to eat, and a legend does not necessarily provide enough to live on.

O.B.'s estate was wound up and probate granted. Hugo, the residuary legatee, signed the documents and took the money. It was not much – equivalent to about four or five months of O.B.'s living expenses. Hugo transferred it to his own bank account. The grand total of O.B.'s savings of a lifetime was two hundred and ninety-four pounds.

Postscript

The complexity of Browning's character seems to be just as difficult to understand today as it was a century ago to those who knew him. He was blessed with talents of a high order – intelligence, charm, wit, stamina, a gift for friendship and a genuine love of youth – which ought to have given him real success in his chosen profession of teaching. At the same time he was cursed with equal and opposite defects – conceit, sloth, narrowness, insensitivity, a genius for upsetting people and an unpleasant homosexual appetite. Over and over again these got him into trouble and stopped him achieving the prizes his talents deserved. The needle on the balance swings back and forward violently between good and bad, and the problem for the biographer which these contradictions pose is formidable.

In particular, the way in which he continued to collect young men, take them about and show them off after Wilde's imprisonment is quite astounding. Every other man of like temperament fled the country or went to ground at that moment, but Browning – dangerously called Oscar, too – continued to flaunt his inclinations with such an air of innocence that even his enemies were left breathless with astonishment. How could he have taken such risks, one asks oneself? He himself appears not to have given the matter a thought, or if he did, to consider his patronage at the age of sixty of young sailors and bank clerks, choristers and railwaymen, aged seventeen and less, as nothing but kindly and normal. One reads their letters, so badly written, so touchingly brought to an end with kisses and forget-me-nots and requests for photographs and keepsakes, and begins to believe him. Was he not, after all, simply speaking the truth when he told his friends, as he often did, of his innocent pride in helping these young fellows? Yet there is no doubt from the contents of some of their letters that his enthusiasm for them led him on many occasions to more than fatherly embraces.

In spite of the great advance in understanding of human behaviour since Browning died in 1923, and all that therefore may be gleaned and deduced from his letters today which ought to provide enough for a sympathetic, comprehensive and harmonious portrait, his character remains largely inexplicable. Nothing can improve the verdict given in 1924 in *Memories and Friends* by his old pupil and colleague, Arthur Benson, who knew him intimately. He wrote, 'It is difficult for those who knew O.B., and it would be impossible for those who did not know him, to disentangle the essential elements of a career and a temperament so extraordinary . . . Oscar Browning was a man of whom it may be fairly said that if his deeds and words were truly and literally reported, the picture would be held to be incredible.'

So we are left with a mystery after all: with a man of extraordinary personal magnetism who repelled or attracted violently, according to polarity, who was detested by some, such as Dr Hornby and loved with an equal intensity by others, as in the case of many of his students at Cambridge.

One of these last may have the final say, and speak for all of his admirers. He is Thomas Anton Bertram, an undergraduate at Caius, with whom Browning had an entirely normal, friendly and unsexual relationship. Over a period of thirty years, Bertram wrote 114 very ordinary, rather boring letters to Browning. In one of them he summed it all up in two words. He was staying by the sea in a boarding house with his mother and sister during the long vacation, and hating it. So he decided to write to Oscar Browning to cheer himself up, just as he had done on many other occasions.[1] This time, however, he did not begin in the usual way with 'Dear Mr Browning', or 'Dear Sir', or 'Dear Tutor', but unexpectedly with two other words which were quite different. He dated the paper first – 'Brighton, 30.8.91'. Then he started the letter. He began, 'Beloved O.B.'

DROPPING THE PILOT.

(With apologies to Sir John Tenniel.)

Pusey on masturbation

Victorian society was obsessed with the supposed dangers of masturbation at this time, and no group more so than those in charge of young men at public schools and universities. In Browning's Archive (O.B. 3/7) is a printed copy of a sermon by E.B. Pusey (himself an Old Etonian) on this subject. Preached to the 'Younger Members of the University' at St Mary's Church, Oxford, on Friday evening, March 1st 1861, entitled, 'The Thought of the Love of Jesus for us, the Remedy for Sins of the Body', it testifies to some of Pusey's personal experiences with this problem.

> But in the trial itself, especially in that sort which (those whom it concerns will know what I mean) comes when no one is by . . . I know but of one effectual remedy – to clasp the hands together, and pray earnestly to God for help . . . Fearful and common those punishments are, which I have seen and known and read of. I have known of manifold early death; I have seen the fineness of intellect injured; powers of reasoning, memory impaired; nay, insanity oftentime, idiotcy; every form of decay of mind and body; consumption too often, torturing death, even of a strong frame. Lesser degrees of these punishments were God's warning voice: at first bodily growth checked, eyesight perhaps distressed or impaired; that fine, beautiful delicate system which carries sensation through the whole human frame, in whatever degree, harmed, and for the most part, in that degree irreparably. When these warnings were neglected, further decay, with scarce an exception, visibly followed . . . That prayer with hands clasped to God I never knew to fail, for God was not called to aid in vain. If the trial lasted, the victory was more complete. I knew one, now many years ago, who, under an almost supernatural power of temptation, had to pray to God, not thrice only, but for seven days and six nights, and at the end, the temptation left him as though it had never been and he told me afterwards it did not return again.

Drawings, paintings, sculptures and caricatures of Oscar Browning

1868	Simeon Solomon; drawing	Original untraced. Reproduced in O.B.'s *Memories of Sixty Years*
1868	Simeon Solomon; drawing	Original untraced. Reproduced in H.E. Wortham's *Oscar Browning*
1868	Albert Bruce Joy; medallion	Now missing. Exhibited at the Royal Academy, 1868, catalogue number 1070
c.1870	William Story; medallion	Now missing. Reproduced in O.B.'s *Memories of Sixty Years*
c.1870	C. Chapman; portrait	Now missing. Given by O.B. to Lord Curzon, 1916. 'Has been mistaken for a Watts.' Letter from O.B. to Curzon, Jan 2nd 1916. (India Office Library, IOR. MSS.Eur.F.111.)
?1887	G.H. Teague; portrait	Presented to Eton College by Lord Latymer, 1922. O.B.'s entry in the D.N.B. refers (1922–1930 Supplement). See also H.E. Wortham's *Oscar Browning*, p. 303.
1888	W.B. Hayes; caricature	'O.B.' *Vanity Fair*, November 24th. Original untraced.
c.1892	Max Beerbohm; caricature	'Mr Oscar Browning.' Collection, Robert H. Taylor, Princeton, N.J.
1900	I. Zuloaga; portrait	Possession of King's College, Cambridge.

Appendix B

1902	'TAB'; caricature	'Dropping the Pilot'. *The Granta*, June 4th. Original untraced.
1903	Lowes Dickinson; portrait	Possession of the Cambridge Union Debating Society.
1908	Max Beerbohm; caricature	'Mid-term tea at Mr Oscar Browning's.' Possession of King's College, Cambridge.
1914	Colin Gill; portrait	Possession of King's College, Cambridge.
1917	Artist unknown; portrait	Now missing. Given by O.B. to the Hastings Public Library. Letter from O.B. to his great-niece, Hester Booth, 19.6.1917 (Booth family archives).
1918	Gwendolen Williams; sculpture	Now missing. Exhibited at The Royal Academy, 1918. Catalogue number 1543.
c.1920	H. Lerche; head, bronze	Possession of the Department of Education, Cambridge University. Reproduced in H.E. Wortham's *Oscar Browning*. O.B.'s *Memories of Later Years*, p. 178, refers.
1921	Naum Los; bust, bronze	Possession of King's College, Cambridge. O.B.'s *Memories of Later Years*, p. 178, refers.
1922	E. Gliecenstein; portrait	Original untraced. Reproduced in O.B.'s *Memories of Later Years*.
1923	E. Gliecenstein; portrait, with valet and dog	Possession of I. Anstruther.
1923	E. Gliecenstein; drawing	Possession of I. Anstruther. Reproduced in Peter Searby's *The Training of Teachers* (Cambridge University, Department of Education, 1982).

Notes

CHAPTER I (pp 5–11)

1 In the first half of this book which deals with Oscar Browning's time at Eton, the word 'Tutor' with a capital 'T' denotes a master who kept a boarding house; the word 'tutor' with a small 't' denotes a master who gave tutorials. It was often the case that a boy's Tutor was also his tutor – a rather confusing arrangement.
2 Issue, April–October 1835, p. 99
3 The first reference to this verse appears to be in a letter to O.B. from Frank N. Curzon (younger brother of George) written on paper headed 'Vincent's Club. Oxford', dated 'Mar.6.87': 'George tells me you have never heard of, or seen, the Epigram consisting of 4 lines, which was composed last year, I think, by H.B. Ottley of Trinity, upon yourself; so here you are.' Interestingly, the H.B. Ottley referred to cannot be traced as an undergraduate at either Trinity College, Oxford, or Cambridge. The letter is in the Browning archive, O.B. 1/444

CHAPTER II (pp 12–19)

1 G.L.C. Microfilm, X30/12
2 G.L.C. Microfilm, X30/62
3 Browning archive (B.A.), O.B. 1/405
4 B.A., O.B. 3/7

CHAPTER III (pp 20–44)

1 B.A., O.B. 2/124
2 All the letters from Sir Charles Murray and from his son quoted in this chapter are in the Browning archive, O.B. 1/1171
3 Both letters from William Story quoted in this chapter are in the Browning archive, O.B. 1/1574
4 See Appendix A
5 B.A., O.B. 2/1
6 Both letters from R.H. Whiteway quoted in this chapter are in the Browning archive, O.B. 1/1749
7 Both letters from Rose Carden quoted in this chapter are in the Browning archive, O.B. 1/313
8 Page 25
9 See Appendix A
10 National Library of Scotland, Main Index. Vol. II, Blackie letters, Folio 279, MSS 2628
11 John Stuart Blackie, *Letters to his Wife*, Ed. A.S. Walker, 1910. p. 176
12 B.A., O.B. 1/401–403
13 The Scottish Record Office: The Balfour papers, Folio 237

CHAPTER IV (pp 45–54)

1 William Johnson (Cory). His journal quoted in this chapter is with the Halsdon MSS in the Library of Eton College. The letters referred to and quoted in this chapter are in the Browning archive, O.B 1/405
2 All the letters from Dr Goodford quoted in this chapter are in the Browning archive, O.B. 1/654
3 B.A., O.B. 1/1570
4 B.A., O.B. 1/18

Notes

CHAPTER V (pp 55–66)

1 All the letters from Simeon Solomon quoted and referred to in this chapter (except the last) are in the Browning archive, O.B. 1/1531. The last is in the British Library, Department of Manuscripts, Ashley 1755
2 Joseph Leftwich MSS, Jerusalem State Archive
3 *Paederastia Apologia.* Anon. Pub. J.W. Arrowsmith, Bristol. No date. B.A., O.B. 3/8
4 The Curzon papers, the India Office Library. MSS.EUR.F.111. Additional papers

CHAPTER VI (pp 67–80)

1 All letters of support for Browning, quoted in the following pages, have been drawn from Printed papers in Eton College Library.
2 B.A., O.B. 3/6
3 B.A., O.B. 1/445–449

CHAPTER VII (pp 81–92)

1 B.A., O.B. 1/1728–1729
2 B.A., O.B. 1/58–65
3 Political Society Minute Book. Library, King's College
4 His essay on Oscar Browning in *Portraits*
5 B.A., O.B. 1/1600
6 Cambridge University Library, Cam.C.877.17
7 University of Leeds, Brotherton Collection
8 B.A., O.B. 1/726

CHAPTER VIII (pp 93–102)

1 B.A., O.B. 1/1204
2 B.A., O.B. 1/1600
3 B.A., O.B. 1/395–397
4 B.A., O.B. 1/1212
5 B.A., O.B. 1/226

6 B.A., O.B. 1/340
7 B.A., O.B. 1/601
8 B.A., O.B. 2/131
9 B.A., O.B. 1/37
10 B.A., O.B. 1/329
11 B.A., O.B. 2/45
12 B.A., O.B. 1/1472
13 B.A., O.B. 2/27
14 B.A., O.B. 2/44

CHAPTER IX (pp 103–120)

1 B.A., O.B. 2/34
2 B.A., O.B. 1/79
3 Rosebery archives, The National Library of Scotland, Edinburgh
4 B.A., O.B. 2/129
5 B.A., O.B. 1/1420
6 June 16 1892
7 November 25 1899
8 B.A., O.B. 2/19
9 A.C. Benson's Diary, vol. 65, Magdalene College, Cambridge
10 A.C. Benson's Diary, vol. 66, Magdalene College, Cambridge
11 B.A., O.B. 1/767
12 B.A., O.B. 1/957
13 November 23 1895
14 November 30 1895
15 May 24 1899
16 January 28 1899
17 January 23 1892
18 November 30 1895
19 May 15 1897
20 October 27 1894

CHAPTER X (pp 121–137)

1 All the letters from O.B.'s mother quoted in this chapter are in the Browning archive, O.B. 1/233
2 B.A., O.B. 1/1681
3 All the letters from Mariana (Dick) Browning quoted in this chapter are in the Browning archive, O.B. 1/234–240
4 All letters from Malvina (Mina) Wortham quoted in

this chapter are in the Browning archive, O.B. 1/1826–1829

5 All the letters from Biscoe Wortham quoted in this chapter are in the Browning archive, O.B. 1/1820–1822

6 B.A., O.B. 1/1393

CHAPTER XI (pp 138–148)

1 B.A., O.B. 1/1250
2 B.A., O.B. 1/863
3 B.A., O.B. 1/1393
4 A.C. Benson's Diary, vol. 65, Magdalene College, Cambridge
5 B.A., O.B. 2/127
6 All the letters from Willie Barrable and his father quoted in this chapter are in the Browning archive, O.B. 1/102–104
7 B.A., O.B. 1/1515–1517

CHAPTER XII (pp 149–162)

1 B.A., O.B. 1/1484
2 University of Cambridge. Department of Education Archives, Box 101
3 Report for 1899/1900, p. 345
4 B.A., O.B. 3/1. Letter dated June 8 1897
5 Both the letters from S.S. Fletcher quoted in this chapter are in the Browning archive, O.B. 1/578–586
6 *Julius Caesar*. Act V, Sc. 4. Dockerill did not quote this quite correctly
7 B.A., O.B. 2/64
8 All the letters from J.R. Jones and his brother quoted in this chapter are in the Browning archive, O.B. 1/887
9 B.A., O.B. 3/8. Frank Money had assumed the additional name of Coutts in 1880

CHAPTER XIII (pp 163–179)

1 B.A., O.B. 1/1452
2 B.A., O.B. 1/269
3 B.A., O.B. 1/1352
4 B.A., O.B. 1/1011
5 B.A., O.B. 3/2
6 A.C. Benson's Diary, vol. 46, Magdalene College, Cambridge
7 B.A., O.B. 1/1158
8 B.A., O.B. 1/1161
9 *Oscar Browning* by H.E. Wortham. Constable & Co. London 1927, p 312. I am indebted to Patrick Wilkinson, Fellow of King's College, for the translation of this poem which, in Wortham's book, is in Latin.

CHAPTER XIV (pp 180–188)

1 Letter from O.B. to Nathaniel Wedd, January 13 1916. King's College Library
2 H.M. Library, Windsor Castle RA CC47/577
3 Letter from O.B. to Sir Charles Webster, February 13 1914. King's College Library
4 Letter from O.B. to G. Lowes Dickinson, May 9 1916. King's College Library
5 *Superior Person*, Kenneth Rose, 1969
6 Letter Oscar Browning to Professor E.G. Browne, January 22 1923. From the Papers of E.G. Browne presented to the University Library, Cambridge, by his Family, 4 August 1981

POSTSCRIPT (pp 189–190)

1 B.A., O.B. 1/143–145

Bibliography and sources

Printed Books

A great number of books on different subjects have to be read in background study for a biography of this kind. (Books by Browning, alone, including those to which he wrote prefaces, or edited, number more than sixty.) In this case, they have ranged from the growth of the British Public School as a social phenomenon; to the history of the Aesthetic Movement; to the change in popular opinion towards homosexuality; to the establishment of compulsory, primary education in England and Wales. It is hard to decide which should be mentioned. In this bibliography I have limited the number to those on two subjects only: Eton College during the 1860s and 1870s; and Cambridge and King's College from the 1880s onwards. The list, otherwise, would be too long. The place of publication is London unless otherwise stated.

Eton
Ainger, A.C., *Eton sixty years ago*, 1917.
Bankes, G.N., *A Day of my life*, 1877.
   An Eton boy's letters, 1901.
Benson, A.C., *Fasti Etonenses* (R.I. Drake, Eton), 1899.
   The Myrtle Bough, privately printed, Eton, 1903.
   Memories and Friends, 1924.
Coleridge, G., *Eton in the 'seventies'*, 1912.
Cornish, F.W., *William Cory – Letters and Journals*, 1897.
An Etonian, *Recollections of Eton*, 1870.
Fletcher, C.R.L., *Edmond Warre*, 1922.
James, M.R., *Eton and King's*, 1926.
Johnson, W. (Cory), *Hints for Eton Masters*, 1898.
Lyte, H.C.M., *A History of Eton College*, 1889.
Lyttleton, E., *Memories and Hopes*, 1925.
Mackenzie, F.C., *William Cory*, 1950.
Macnaghten, H., *Fifty years at Eton*, 1924.
Maude, J., *Memories*, privately printed, 1936.

Bibliography

Nevill, R., *Floreat Etona*, 1911.

Richards, J.B., *Seven years at Eton*, 1883.

Rose, K., *Superior Person*, 1969.

Salt, H.S., *Eton under Hornby*, 1910.

Seventy years among Savages, 1921.

Memories of bygone Eton, 1928.

Welldon, J.E.C., *Recollections and Reflexions*, 1915.

Cambridge

Benson, E.F., *As we were*, 1930.

Browning, O., *Memories of Sixty Years*, 1910.

Memories of Later Years, 1923.

Dalton, E.H.J.N., *Call back yesterday*, 1953.

Fitzgerald, M.H., *A Memoir of H.E. Ryle*, 1928.

Furbank, P.N., E.M. *Forster: A Life*, 1977.

Leigh, A.A., *King's College* (Cambridge), 1899.

Leslie, J.R.S., *The Film of Memory*, 1938.

Long Shadows, 1966.

Levy, P., *Moore*, 1979.

MacCarthy, D., *Portraits*, 1931.

Newsome, D., *On the Edge of Paradise*, 1980.

Pfaff, R.W., *Montague Rhodes James*, 1980.

Proctor, D. (editor), *The Autobiography of G. Lowes Dickinson*, 1973.

Raverat, G., *Period Piece*, 1952.

Rothblatt, S., *The Revolution of the Dons*, 1968.

Santayana, G., *My Host the World*, 1953.

Stratford, E.C.W., *Before the Lamps went out*, 1945.

Wilkinson, L.P., *A Century of King's* (Cambridge), 1980.

Wormell, D., *Sir John Seeley and the Uses of History* (Cambridge), 1980.

Wortham, H.E., *Oscar Browning*, 1927.

Periodicals

Edinburgh Review, 1830, 1831

Quarterly Review, 1834, 1860

Quarterly Journal of Education, 1834, 1835

Westminster Review, 1835

Cornhill Magazine, 1860, 1861

Eton College Chronicle, 1864–1875

Bibliography

The Saturday Review, 1875, 1889
The Cambridge Review, 1880–1910
The Cambridge University Reporter, 1880–1910
The Granta, 1889–1910
Etoniana, 1952, 1955
Historical Journal, 1973

Printed Reports

Report of Her Majesty's Commissioners appointed to inquire into the revenues and management of certain colleges and schools . . . 1864.

Hansard's Parliamentary Debates, 1876.

The Fourteenth Report on Public Petitions, Appendix, 1876.

Annual Reports of the Committee of Council on Education (England and Wales), 1890–1900.

Printed Papers in Eton College Library

Correspondence between the Right Honorable E.H. Knatchbull-Hugessen, M.P., and Dr Hornby . . . 1875.

Memorial from E.H. Knatchbull-Hugessen to The Governing Body of Eton College, 1875.

Memorial from sixty-two parents to The Governing Body of Eton College, 1875.

Letters from sixty-two parents to Dr Hornby, 1875.

Letters received from Colleagues and others by Oscar Browning, Esq., 1875.

Letters from Dr Hornby to The Governing Body of Eton College stating, '. . . the circumstances which have led to Mr Browning's dismissal.' 1875.

Memorial from Oscar Browning to The Governing Body of Eton College, '. . . in support of my application to you for a pension . . .' 1875.

Bibliography

Memorial from Oscar Browning to The Governing Body of Eton College, '. . . informing you that I do not admit Dr Hornby's legal right to dismiss me . . .' 1875.

Pamphlets in Eton College Library

Some Remarks on the present studies . . . of Eton School. 1834.
The Eton abuses considered. 1834.
A few words in reply to 'Some remarks . . .' 1834.
The Eton system of education vindicated . . . 1834.
The Harcourt Collection of Etoniana
The Hambleden Collection of Etoniana

University Library, Cambridge

The Clark Collection of Cambridge books and ephemera
The Cambridge Papers (Historical Library, F.A. 4528)

MSS & MS collections

The Oscar Browning Papers	East Sussex County Library, Lewes
The Blackie Letters	National Library of Scotland
The Blackwood Papers	ditto
The Rosebery Papers	ditto
The Balfour Papers	National Register of Archives (Scotland)
The Brotherton Collection	University of Leeds
The Prothero Papers	D.M.S. Watson Library, Royal Historical Society
The Diaries of A.C. Benson	Magdalene College, Cambridge
The Archives of the Department of Education	University of Cambridge

Bibliography

The Woolf Papers	University of Sussex
Letters from O.B. to George Eliot, and others	Yale University Library
Letters from O.B. to the Secretary of the Public Schools Commission, 1862/63	The Public Record Office, HO. 73/58/1
Minutes of the Cambridge Union Debating Society, 1858, 1859; 1880–1904	Cambridge Union Archives
Minutes of the Epicurean Debating Society (St. John's College)	Hamilton Thompson family archives
Minutes of the Eton Literary Society, 1871	Eton College Library
Minutes of the Eton Society (Pop), 1855	ditto
Minutes of the Governing Body of Eton College, 1874, 1875	ditto
Journal of William Johnson (Halsdon MSS), 1863–1869	ditto
Journal of E.C. Austen Leigh, 1875, 1876	ditto
Journal of E.W. Hamilton (Harcourt Collection, B/2.10.), 1863	ditto
Letters, A.W.M. Clark-Kennedy, 1865, 1867	Clark-Kennedy family archives
Autobiography, A. Cooke-Yarborough (Unpublished), 1864	Cooke-Yarborough family archives
Diary of J.T. Sheppard	King's College Library, Cambridge
Memoirs of N. Wedd	ditto
'The University', N. Wedd	ditto
Minutes of the Political Society (King's College), 1876–1908	ditto

Bibliography

Letters in King's College Library, Cambridge

Roger Fry to his mother
E.M. Forster to his mother
O.B. to E.M. Forster, J.M. Keynes, N. Wedd, C. Webster, G.L. Dickinson, J.T. Sheppard

OFF TO THE FRONT!

(Mr. Oscar Browning is in Sympathy with the Boers.)

Index

Acton, Lord, 107, 185
Adey, More, 137, 139
Aesthetic Movement, 55, 57
Ainger, A.C., 78; on O.B., 52–3
Albert, Prince Consort, 15
Ambrose, Sewell, 141
Anderson, Robert, 100
Anstruther, Ralph, 75
Anstruther, Sir Robert, 75
Antinori, Ettore, 181, 186
Argyll, Duke of, 120
Arnold, Dr Thomas, 18, 39
Arrowsmith, Rev William, 12
Austen, Jane, 75
Austen Leigh, E.C., 149, 158; letter
  to O.B., 84–5

Bacon, William; letter to O.B., 103
Bailey, George, 141
Balfour, A.J.; letter to O.B., 106–7
Balfour, Gerald, 57–9; O.B. on,
  43–4; letter to O.B., 70
Balliol College, Oxford, 104
Balston, Dr Thomas, 35, 52
Barker, John, 141
Barnes, George, 76, 78
Barrable, Willie, 142–6; letters to
  O.B., 143–4
Benson, A.C., The Myrtle Bough,
  quoted, 40; on O.B., 113–4, 140,
  174, 187, 190
Bertram, T.A., 190
Binney (Wortham's pupil), 129–31
Blackie, Professor J.S.; letter to O.B.,
  41–2
Bliss, Sidney, 141
Brand, Frederick, 99
Bromsgrove Messenger, 110
Brooke, Rupert, 171
Brown, Albert; letters to O.B., 98–9
Browne, Professor E.G.; O.B.'s letter
  to, 185

Browning, Arthur (O.B.'s brother),
  121
Browning, Frederick (O.B.'s
  nephew), 121, 128
Browning, Malvina ('Mina', O.B.'s
  sister), see Wortham
Browning, Mariana (O.B.'s
  mother), 12–14, 69, 73, 82, 93,
  133; travels with O.B., 16–17,
  37–8, 76–7; with O.B. at Eton, 18,
  26, 35, 38, 74; death (1889), 121–5;
  132; character, 39–40, 42; letters
  to O.B., 122–4; O.B.'s verses to,
  186
Browning, Mariana ('Dick', O.B.'s
  sister), 38, 40, 42, 69, 73–4, 129,
  131–3; travels with O.B., 16–18,
  37–8, 76–7; as headmistress,
  125–7; O.B. at Bexhill with, 175;
  death (1910), 176; letters to O.B.,
  126–7
Browning, Oscar (1837–1923); early
  life, 12–13; as Eton Scholar,
  13–16; as undergraduate, 17–19;
  as President Cambridge Union,
  18; assistant master at Eton
  (1860–61), 18, 20, 45; Wm.
  Johnson (Cory) on, 45–6;
  meetings of United Ushers, 150;
  housemaster at Eton (1862), 9,
  22–3, 38–41; dismissed from Eton,
  5–9, 65–6, 68–80 passim; letter to
  Provost, 73; as don at Cambridge,
  9, 10, 80, 81–92 passim; as founder
  Political (Historical) Society,
  85–7, 169; as founder Musical
  Society, 87; as Liberal candidate,
  108–11; success at Cambridge,
  102, 104, 111–20 passim; mother's
  death, 121, 124–5; family troubles,
  125–37; life in London, 141–5; as
  Principal Day Training College,

149–62 *passim*; visits India, 165; disappointments at Cambridge, 166–71; retirement, 174–9; in Rome during World War I, 180–84; awarded OBE, 184; death, 186; cremation, 184, 186; memorial service, 187; appearance, 113–15; view of athleticism, 39, 61; Commission of Inquiry, 46; as educator, 150–7 *passim*; as friend of youth, 93–101, 141–8; and 'Greek Love', 56, 58–9; as historian, 102–6, 170; knowledge of languages, 186; letters to, 9; love of music, 16–17, 185–6; love of nobility and royalty, 16, 29, 117–19, 181–2; as reformer, 46–52, 68, 91; as scholar, 107, 182; self-indulgence of, 42; and sexual morality, 32, 35, 40–41, 56, 61; as teacher, 21, 38–9, 41, 51–4; travels abroad, 16, 29, 31, 37–8, 42–3, 57, 69–70, 92; treatment of favourites, 30–33, 46; as tutor, 21–2, 65; as Tutor (housemaster), 23, 39–41; ungenerous to sister, 126–7; verses by, 175, 178; as writer, 102, 104; publications, 41, 102; *The Age of the Condottieri*, 105; *Charles XII*, 105, 117; *Flight to Varennes*, 104, 168–9; *A General History of the World*, 182; *Goëthe*, 117; *Guelphs and Ghibellines*, 105, 117; *A History of the Modern World*, 182; *Life of George Eliot*, 104, 168; *Memories of Sixty Years*, 6, 31, 38, 58, 155, 165, 175–6, 190; *A New Illustrated History of England*, 102, 106; *Peter the Great*, 105, 117; *A Short History of Italy*, 182;

Browning, Robert, 29, 92, 112
Browning, Rev William (O.B.'s brother), 13
Buckland, Charles; letters to O.B., 164–5
Butcher, S.H.; letter to O.B., 70
Butler, Dr H.M., letter to O.B., 69–70

Cambridge Review, 175
Cambridge Teachers' Training Syndicate, 151, 174
Cambridge Training College for Women, 156
Cambridge University, 17–19; the Apostles, 18, 85; the Epicureans, 111; Political (Historical) Society, 85–6; Union Society, 18, 74, 166–7, 187
Cambridge University Day Training College, 152–62
Campbell, Freddie; letter to O.B., 142
Campbell, William, 141
Carden, Arthur, 36–7
Carden, Mrs Rose, 35; letters to O.B., 36–7
Chamberlain, Austen, 86, 108–10, 112, 175
Chamberlain, Joseph, 108
Charterhouse School, 74
Cheltenham College, 7
Chivers, Stanley, 99
Christian Science, 183, 186
Clarence, Duke of, 117–18
Clark-Kennedy, W.M., 20
Clarke, A.H., 177
Clarke, W.C.; verses to O.B., 178–9
Clifton College, 150
Copeman, Alfred, 95, 97
Copeman, Charlie, 94–5, 97
Cornish, Blanche, 78
Cornish, Frank Warre, 17, 78; letters to O.B., 42, 50, 70; O.B.'s verses to, 175–6
Cory, William, *see* Johnson
Curzon, George Nathaniel (1st Marquess Curzon), 6, 10, 62–5, 71–2, 75–8; as Viceroy, 163–5; letter to O.B., 79–80; O.B.'s letter to, 184. *See also* Scarsdale

Daily News, 72
Dansey, C., 133–4, 136
Dickinson, Goldsworthy Lowes, 171; O.B.'s letter to, 183

Dickinson, Lowes (father of G.L.D.), 166, 187
Dockerill, Harry, 159
Douglas, Lord Alfred, 135, 138
Drew, Admiral, A., 23
Dublin Daily Independent, 109

Eggesford Rectory, 127–32
Eglinton Tournament, 38
Eighty Club, 103, 111
Eliot, George, 41, 64, 91–2, 187
Ellis, Miriam, 177
Eton College, 8, 74; Boating Song, 45; Choir, 46–9, 73; education at, 20–22; Eton Society ('Pop'), 16, 39, 78; games and sport, 78; Literary Society, 39, 61; reforms recommended by Commission, 46–7; Scholars, 14, 17; 'sets', 45–6; sexual immorality, 8, 13–14; tutors, 5–8, 21–2, 65; Tutors (housemasters), 6, 23, 39–41; O.B.'s dismissal, 5–6, 65–6, 68–80 *passim*, 81; O.B.'s salary, 22–3

Farrar, Dean, 120
Fechheimer (Fletcher) Dr Sigmund, 156–7; letters to O.B., 157–8
Fettes School, 41
Forster, E.M., 171, 185
Fox, Charlie, 99
Fullerton, David, 36

Gladstone, Mrs, 122
Gladstone, William, 5, 92, 108, 113, 120
Gliecenstein, Emanuel, 186
Goodford, Dr C.O. ('The Cogger'), 18, 73, 81; letters to O.B., 47–9
Granta, The, 111–13, 115–19, 166
'Greek Love', 55–66 *passim*, 138
Green, George, 13
Guardian, The, 105
Gull, Sir William, 38

Haileybury School, 8
Hammond, B.E., 92
Harrow School, 8, 37, 69, 74, 122

Hayes, W.B., 114
Hayne, Rev Dr L.G., 48–9
Henley, 78
Hinton, Howard; letter to O.B., 110–11
Hodgson, Francis, 85
Home Rule, 109, 111
Homfrey, Rev. W., 31
Hornby, Rev Dr J.J., 5–10, 52–3, 61, 81, 122; dismisses O.B., 64–6, 71–3; background and character, 67–8
Hornby, Sir Phipps, 67
Houghton, Lord (Richard Moncton Milnes), 41, 57
Hughes, Miss (Cambridge Training College for Women), 156
Hyde, Albert, 100

Iliffe, Mr (Day Training College), 155–6
Ives, George, 145

Jackson, R.C.; letter to O.B., 139
James, M.R., 158
Jex-Blake, Dr T.W., 151
Johnson (Cory), William, 8, 17; on O.B., 14, 51; as teacher, 15, 21; friendship with O.B., 45–7, 50; dismissed, 60–61
Jones, J.R., 159; letters to O.B., 160–62
Jowett, Professor B., 114, 139; letter to O.B., 104

Keate, Dr John, 10, 13
Keynes, J.M., 171, 185
Kidman, Frederick, 101
King's College, Cambridge, 8–9, 118; O.B. as undergraduate, 17; O.B. as Fellow, 81–92 *passim*; O.B. on his contribution, 185
Knatchbull-Hugessen, E.H., 7, 65, 72–5
Kummer, Charles, 141

Lamb, Archie, 38
Lamb, Charlie, 38

Index

Latymer, *see* Money
Lawrence, George, 57
Leeland, Samuel; letter to O.B., 101
Le Marchant, Latimer, 38
Little, J.F., 113
Longfellow, Henry, 29
Lord's Cricket Ground, 67, 78
Luxmoore, H.E., 78
Lyons, Francis, 101

MacCarthy, Desmond; on O.B.'s 'at homes', 88–9
Macaulay, W.H., 168, 170
Manning, Cardinal, 120
Marlborough College, 7
Mary, Queen, 119; O.B.'s letter to, 181–2
Maxse, Leo, 86
Michaelides, Constantine, 173–4
Millais, John, 120
Money (Money-Coutts, Lord Latymer), Frank *or* Francis, 77–8, 140–41, 162; letters to O.B., 71, 139
Morning Post, 72
Morris, Herbert Picton ('Bertie'), 38
Morris, William, 56, 92
Motley, J.L., 29
Moxon, Henry; letter to O.B., 175
Murray, Sir Charles; letters to O.B., 24–28
Muscular Christianity, 10

Nicolson, Sir Arthur, 178
Nixon, J.E., 93–5, 97

Oates, Matthew, 95–7, 134
Okes, Dr R., 81, 90
Oliver, Augusta Ann, 176
Ottley, H.B.; on O.B., 10

Pater, Walter, 41, 56–7, 59, 61, 139
Palairet, Charlie, 32–3
Paton, William ('Poodle'); letter to O.B., 138
Pear's Encyclopaedia, 179
Platonic love, 55
Pleasance, Spencer, 101

Portsmouth, Lord, 77, 127–9; letter to O.B., 71
Potts, T. Todd, 177
Prothero, (Sir) George, 149; letter to O.B., 83–4
public schools, 8, 18, 68; Parliamentary Commission of Inquiry (1864), 20–21, 46; 'Greek Love', 56
Public Schools Act (1868), 74; Petition against, 74–5
Pusey, E.B., 40, 114, 191

Quarterly Journal of Education, 7
Queen's Scholarships, 152–4, 159

Reid, J.S., 169
Rosebery, Lord, 107
Ross, Robbie, 96–7, 133–7, 140; letters to O.B., 136, 139–40
Rossetti, Dante Gabriel, 56
Rugby School, 18, 39, 74, 151
Ruskin, John, 61, 120

Salisbury, Lord, 120
Scarsdale, 4th Baron, 6, 62, 78
Schuster, Lady Isabella; letter to O.B., 23–4
Secondé, Emile; letter to O.B., 163–4
Seeley, Sir John, 84, 104, 107
Selwyn, J.R., 122; letter to O.B., 100
Shelton, Percy, 100–101
Sheppard, J.T., 97, 185
Shrewsbury School, 74
Sidgwick, Arthur, 150
Sidgwick, Henry, 17
Simpson, Edgar, 146–7
Sleigh, Herbert, 184
Smith, Featonby, 142, 145–6; letter to O.B., 147–8
Spiritualism, 124, 186
Solomon, Simeon, 55–6, 139, 187; letters to O.B., 57–60
Standard, 72
Stanley, H.M., 120
Stellmann, Hermann, 141
Stephen, J.K., 118
Stone, E.D., 80; letter to O.B., 50–51

Story, Julian, 29–32, 57
Story, Waldo, 29–32, 38
Story, William, 29, 38, 39, 187–8;
  letters to O.B., 30, 31
Stuart, Gertrude, 177
Sturge, P.H., 86
Sullivan, Sir Arthur, 41
Sutcliffe, Wallace, 141
Sutherland-Gower, Lord Ronald,
  141–2
Swinburne, Algernon, 56–7, 60, 187;
  O.B. on, 58
Symonds, J.A., 89–90, 95, 104, 139

Teague, G.H., 187
Teck family, 119
Tenniel, Sir John, 166
Tennyson, Alfred Lord, 61, 120, 187
Thackeray, W.M., 29
The Times, 72, 176
Tom Brown's Schooldays, 39
Trevelyan, G.M., 17, 184
Trevelyan, Sir G.O., 176
Trinity College, Cambridge, 17, 82,
  84, 89, 92, 108, 118
Trollope, Anthony, 29
Turnor, Lady Caroline, 24

Udall, Nicholas, 5
University College School, 75

Vanity Fair, 114–15, 120, 121
Vassall, Oliver, 77
Victoria, Queen, 15, 24, 117

Waldstein, Dr Charles, 117–18;
  letter to O.B., 124–5

Warre, Edmond, 38
Webster, (Sir) Charles; letter from
  O.B., 182–3
Wedd, Nathaniel; on O.B., 173–4;
  letter from O.B., 181
Welldon, J.E.C., 122; letter to O.B.,
  82–3
Wellington College, 7
Westminster School, 8, 74
Whiteway, R.H.; letters to O.B.,
  33–5
Whitting, Fred, 149
Wilde, Oscar, 96, 103, 120, 138–40,
  187, 189; *Ballad of Reading Gaol*,
  140; *Picture of Dorian Gray*, 142
Wilson, H.G., 155
Wilson, James, 89
Wilson, J.M., 150
Winchester College, 8, 20, 74
Wolley-Dod, Rev, C., 6, 62, 64
World, The, 120
World War I (1914–18), 180
Wortham, Rev. Biscoe, 127–37
  passim, 180
Wortham, Dorothea, 129
Wortham, Hugo (O.B.'s nephew), 6,
  14, 59, 97–8, 184, 187–8
Wortham, Malvina ('Mina', O.B.'s
  sister, *nee* Browning), 38, 40, 42,
  69, 73–4, 123; travels with O.B.,
  16–18, 37–8, 76–7; married life,
  127–137 *passim*; letters to O.B.,
  128–9, 134–7; death (1911), 180
Wortham, Oswald ('Toddy'), 129,
  134–7
Wortham, Philip, 129, 133–4, 136

Zuloaga, I., 187